THE NICETIES OF DISTRICT PLANNING

THE NICETIES OF DISTRICT PLANNING

An Operational Framework

Dr. Bedprakas Syam Roy

KALPAZ

The Niceties of District Planning : An Operational Framework

ISBN: 978-81-7835-917-5

Published in 2012 in India by
Kalpaz Publications
C-30, Satyawati Nagar,
Delhi-110052
E-mail: kalpaz@hotmail.com
Phone : 9212729499

Lasser Type Setting by: Rudra Computer Graphics, Delhi
Printed at : Chawla Offset Printers, Delhi

To My Father who wished me to be analytical in approach

Contents

Preface

Decentralisation has been a catchy phrase for all functionaries connected in some way with rural development and district administration. I was aware of theoretical framework of the subject as a student of Economics and later came across its practical meaning with my first posting as a Civil Services Officer in the drought-prone district of Purulia, West Bengal. The decentralisation application at that time (early 1974) was passing through its infant stage of trial and error and was, in a way, in an exploring mode to find the right course of action. Luckily for me, I was associated with the experimentation of the first generation of West Bengal model on decentralisation initiated by late Pannalal Dasgupta, Vice-Chairman of the then State Planning Board, West Bengal and an illustrious icon on applied rural development. This initial exposure impacted me profoundly at my formative stage and got enriched later when I had the hand holding opportunity to work with the implementation of the West Bengal Panchayat Act,1978. I came into contact with the second generation of West Bengal model on decentralisation in 1992 just before the 73rd and the 74th Amendment of the Constitution during my assignment in the Development and Planning department. I happened to be connected with the third generation model with the beginning of the West Bengal District Planning Act,1994 and the West Bengal District Planning, Rules 1994 published as a follow-up to the Constitutional Amendments.

In course of my association with the District Planning related interactions, I have come across, besides Panchayat and Municipal representatives, three types of stake holders, namely, (a) Government functionaries, (b) Development Economists, and (c) Training/Capabilities enhancing functionaries. They are important and influential actors in this area. To my utter bewilderment, however, I have noticed, among them, plural variations on perceptions on basics as well as on its contents on decentralised plan including its process as provided under Article 243ZD, the Eleventh and the Twelfth Schedule, and other related Articles in the Constitution of India. Such understanding differences exist within each segment of the decentralisation community and more particularly among the government functionaries of the State Governments, Central Governments and also in the Planning Commission. The end result is that there is an overcasting cloud of confusion and the decentralised movement in the country, barring a few exceptions, could not make much headway as conceived in the scheme of Constitutional Amendments. The net outcome of this casualty is discernable in the quality of Annual Plans prepared by the local governments in our country.

The Planning Commission being aware of this unhappy state of affairs resolved that with the beginning of the Eleventh Five Year Plan, decentralised planning has to be made a reality by removing all the impediments that have appeared to roadblock the process. Accordingly, the Ministry of Panchayat, Government of India appointed an Expert Group with V. K. Ramchandran as chairperson. The Expert Group presented 'Planning at the Grassroots level' to the Central Government in March 2006 as a model of planning for decentralised local bodies in the country. The Report of the Expert Group was shared with the District Planning Committees and rural local bodies of the country. The Planning Commission also simultaneously issued guidelines on District planning on the basis of the Report of the Expert Group at the beginning of the Eleventh Five Year Plan.

The 'Planning at the Grassroots level' served a very useful role in sensitising the rural local bodies on the modalities of planning and the format of its step by step approach. However, it was not enough for district planning. The areas of urban planning have not been included by the Expert Group nor did it touch upon the functional aspect of consolidation by the District Planning Committee. In the given circumstances, the Planning Commission appointed a Task Force on District Planning Committee and the Manual on District Planning, as prepared by the said Task Force, has been published by the Planning Commission. It retained the basic recommendations on planning as incorporated earlier by the Expert Group at 'Planning at the Grassroots level'.

The Manual on District Planning addressed, in details, aspects of district planning including urban planning and consolidation function of the District Planning Committee. It resolved to address the unmet guidance on preparing draft district plan and qualify as a possible problem solving handbook. However, on close examination, it appeared that the Manual on District Planning has generated a fresh bout of confusion including in the spawning of a different version of consolidation than is permissible in the constitutional scheme of devolution. In the end, the envisaged roadmap for preparing a draft district plan by consolidating plans prepared by the Panchayats and the Municipalities is hardly available from the said Manual. Further, guidelines on district planning issued by the Planning Commission and other ministries of the Government of India (Appendices-3 series) do not have uniformity in approach. Incidentally, no other publication on the said subject area with clearly defined function on consolidation of the District Planning Committee has come to the fore as yet. The Niceties on District Planning-An Operational Framework attempts to fill in this void area by way of meeting constitutional requirement and the basics of planning logic.

In preparing 'The Niceties on District Planning-An Operational Framework', I am indebted to the opportunity I got to work at policy level on decentralisation in course of my services in West Bengal and the scope for interaction with the Decentralisation Community in the UNDP Solution Exchange platform for a number of years. I am grateful to functionaries of District Planning Committees, levels of Panchayats, representatives of the Municipalities and Development Economists who helped me to understand the practical problems connected with decentralised planning and more precisely, the crucial area of consolidation.

I have made liberal use of the publications of Government of India and other documents but do not specifically mention them in view of constraint of space.

I am grateful to Prof. K. Rajasekharan of KILA who helped me a lot to understand the Kerala model of decentralisation and to Dr. P.N. Roy, Former Member, State Planning Board, West Bengal for consultations on conceptual clarifications on certain points.

My daughter, Maniparna, has been my constant source of encouragement and her invaluable assistance deserves special mention.

I am thankful to Kalpaz Publications, Delhi for agreeing to publish the book at the shortest period of time.

Finally, I shall consider my efforts amply rewarded if the publication serves as a reference book on decentralisation and be of useful to prepare draft District Development Plan.

Sept. 2011

Dr. Bedprakas Syam Roy
JC-2, Flat-4, Sector-3, Salt Lake,
Kolkata-700098,

1

Decentralised Planning-the Beginning of New Experiment

Democracy and democratic governance have become the order of the human civilization and are also the very attributes of any modern state. Gone are the days when the citizens of a state looked forward for the amenities of life on the benevolent dictator. It was totally a destiny driven life of inequity and uncertainty. It does no longer fit in with the concept of ownership and participation of the modern mind. It is not the chance factor but opening up of opportunities that characterizes democratic governance. Democratic governance is now the ultimate destination point of all governance system around the world. Its formal structure may vary from one country to another on ground of geo-political and cultural diversity but the inherent fundamental of popular participation is the hall mark of decentralised model of governance everywhere in the world. The traditional system of governance by remote control from distant location is also no substitute for a system of local governance and local participation. The local participation enables not only selection of locally relevant schemes with its bearing on living environment, it also promotes cost efficiency by subjecting openness to public scrutiny and by institutionalizing accountability to the stake holder community and other individuals. Further, involving local people may also result in investment in socially desirable services, particularly in drinking water, health care and primary education and in the process meets development deficit of the locality to a great extent. Additionally, Decentralization can increase economic participation by facilitating local entrepreneurial activity, and thus increasing employment, in several ways.

Decentralised governance may have different character and forms. From an operational angle, it might be divided into two ways (a) horizontal and (b) vertical. Horizontal decentralisation is characterised by dispersal of power among institutions at the same level e.g. decision of any government to concurrently empower its line departments to take spending decisions like those of its finance department belongs to this category. Here financial power is spread across the line departments without keeping it concentrated within the finance department only. Vertical decentralisation is distinguished by delegation of some of the powers of the central government to the lower tier of authorities–to states in federal countries and further down to regional and local governments or even to village institutions.

Vertical decentralization of any government can itself take three forms:

(a) Deconcentration

It is the primary stage of decentralisation where limited power and authority are passed down. It is confined to exercising administrative discretion at the level of local offices of the ministries of the government. In this system although it does take place some dispersal of power, few decisions can be taken without reference to the government.

(b) Delegation

This falls in the intermediate stage of decentralisation where some defined authority and decision-making powers on specified items are passed on to local officials. But the government retains the right to overturn local decisions and can, at any time, take these powers back. Like deconcentration, it is confined to among the officials of the government. It does not cover local level institutions.

(c) Devolution

It is the strongest form of decentralization .It covers local level institutions only. In this form of decentralisation, full decision-making powers are granted to local authorities and allowing them to take full responsibility without reference back to the government. Such bodies are empowered with financial power as well as the authority to design and execute local development projects and programmes. It is also instrumental to pave the way for fiscal decentralisation. In other words, for qualifying devolution there needs to exist three essential requisites namely:

(i) functional autonomy in respect of defined subjects for decision taking

(ii) financial autonomy on resource raising

(iii) implementation autonomy on schemes designed by them.

The Constitution of India, while institutionalising local governance in the country under the Seventy Third and the Seventy Fourth Amendments, adopted this devolution mode of vertical decentralisation as described above and accordingly enshrined ' ..the devolution of powers and responsibilities upon Panchayats, at the appropriate level' under Article 243G and '..the devolution of powers and responsibilities upon Municipalities' under Article 243W. In other words, it is not the old PRIs concept of undivided family and togetherness as such but that all tiers of Panchayat would need to have distinct devolved powers and responsibilities from the Eleventh Schedule, as institutions of self-government. Similarly; the Municipalities need to have distinct devolved powers and responsibilities from the Twelfth Schedule, as institutions of self-government. The quality of democratic governance in our country depends on our ability to follow the constitution mandated path of devolution.

The Constitution of India provided for District Planning Committee under Article 243ZD to consolidate plans prepared by the Panchayats and the Municipalities. The Gram Panchayat, Block Panchayat and Zilla Panchayat have been mandated by the Constitution to prepare Gram Panchayat Plan, Block Panchayat Plan and Zilla Panchayat Plan respectively. Similarly, the Municipal Plan is to be prepared by the concerned municipality. Since planning is linked with ownership and implementation of schemes and is also connected with the very growth of local governments, the Constitution of India has empowered these local bodies with planning function. Since there cannot exist any parallel and duplicate planning function for any other body in the same area, the Constitution of India has empowered the District Planning Committee (DPC) with consolidation function of plans prepared by the Panchayats and the Municipalities. The DPC does not have any independent planning function. This is the format of new experimentation on Decentralised planning in India.

Decentralised Planning Initiatives in India till the Constitutional Amendment: An Historical Account

The ideas and concept of decentralisation as a strategy for rural development in our country are very ancient. It existed even before the advent of the British when the model for rural development was circled around self-contained village economy. After the break-down of the self-contained village economy, the rural country side suffered from dearth of institutional efforts to improve village economy. It was only during the later part of the independence movement when the national leaders in their search for blueprint for economic development for free India diagnosed the merit, prospect and virtue of decentralisation. Notable among all such recommendations were the National Planning Committee(1938), the Bombay Plan (1944), the People's Plan by Sri M.N. Roy, Sri Shriman Narayan's Gandhian Plan (1944) and District Development Scheme: Economic Progress by Forced Marches.

After independence and the heralding of the planning era, decentralisation found expression as a planning strategy in the blueprint of India's First Five Year Plan. It recognised the importance to break up the total planning exercise into National, State, District and Local Community Levels. However, it was not further carried forward and the establishment of Community Development Blocks was intended to take care of multi-dimensional rural development needs. The introduction of the concept of multi-level planning in our planning system was the only high mark of the first edition of our plan.

The Second Five Year Plan introduced the concept of District Development Council and the thought of village plans. It also spoke of popular participation in planning through the process of democratic decentralisation. Here again, in that nascent stage of planning, the avowed ideas remained non functional because of the absence of a properly structured decentralised framework. It was for the same reason that integration of micro-level activities for accelerated development could not take place.

The search for an appropriate democratic decentralised set-up was felt strongly and the Government of India appointed an Expert Committee-popularly known as Balwant Rai Mehta Committee-to go into the working of the Community Development Blocks and its support institutions. It recommended decentralisation of administration and democratisation of power. It suggested three-tier organic Panchayati Raj institutions-the base level institution being the Village Panchayat, overseen by Panchayat Samiti and the Zilla Parihad at the apex in the district. The recommendations were accepted and the States enacted legislations with suitable regional variations. The initial enthusiasm petered out as such institutions were found to be captive with no real authority. The momentum to take off decentralisation was virtually lost.

The Third Five Year Plan was not very noteworthy for any special initiative on decentralisation. A relatively strong focus was, however, noticeable in the Fourth five year plan on the importance of regional, district and local plans. The programme envisaged that the Block plans would be the central focus to connect local initiatives, efforts of the line departments and other socio-economic activities. The absence of any effective planning machinery was again responsible for not having due trial of this model of decentralisation.

The Administrative Reforms Commission in its Report of 1967 observed that district planning needs to be confined to those areas where local variations in the pattern and process of development were likely to yield quick results in terms of growth. It also highlighted the need for placement of fund at the level of district authorities to draw purposeful plan.

The Planning Commission issued guidelines in 1969 on formulating district plan including its concept and methodology for drawing up annual plan, medium term plan and perspective plan .A scheme for strengthening planning machinery at the state level was introduced in 1972-73 under Centrally Sponsored Scheme with cost sharing at 2:1 between the Central and the State Government. The said scheme was extended for the planning machinery at district and sub-district level with a cost sharing basis at 50:50 in 1982-83. While this initiative resulted in preparation of district plans in few forward states, the introduction of area specific and beneficiary oriented schemes made it impossible for an integrated approach in district plan and hence had limited success.

A Working Group on block level planning headed by Prof. M.L. Dantwala submitted a Report in 1978 where it was observed that remoteness from the district headquarter for far away actual scene of action is responsible for the district plan being less pragmatic in allocation of resources for meeting location specific needs. The Working Group strongly recommended that block level planning should be the appropriate sub-state planning level for proper appreciation of the felt needs of the people. In the spirit of the recommendations, Planning Commission issued guidelines on formulation of Block level plans.

Around the same time, a Committee was appointed to go into the working of the Panchayati Raj Institutions with Shri Ashoke Mehta as Chairman. The Committee submitted its Report in 1978. It observed that addressing needs of the poor require a high degree of coordination which is not possible to be achieved at the state level. It recommended block planning and also suggested that Panchayati Raj institutions should be made to develop into agencies capable of planning schemes of immediate necessity.

Planning Commission set up a Working Group on District Planning in September, 1982 with Dr. Hanumantha Rao, Member, Planning Commission as Chairperson. The working Group submitted its Report in May, 1984 and hoped that the report will stimulate further thinking on district planning so that district planning can be taken up by all the states from the first year of the Seventh Plan. The highlights of the major recommendations were the following:

(1) 'At the state level, decisions have to be taken regarding proper sharing of functions between itself and inter-dependency.

(2) Each district plan, though specific to its own agro-climatic and socio-economic conditions, must reflect the basic objectives of the national plan and the divisible outlay may be distributed among the districts on the basis of population, area and the level of development.

(3) There should be District Planning Bodies in which the collector must be the Chief Co-ordinator and which should consist of a Chairman, Member-secretary and about fifty members. The District Planning Cell should be headed by a Chief Planning Officer assisted by Block Level Planning officers and technical experts from various disciplines.

(4) The District Planning Body should function as an umbrella organisation for all agencies in the district, motivating

them to work for the welfare of the district. Dialogue on development between the District Development Agency and the District Planning Board should be institutionalised by providing for representation on each other.

(5) For district planning to succeed, not only functions, powers and finances are to be decentralised but consensus should also be built up. The Working Group recommended a stage by stage approach for achieving the objective of proper district planning.'

A Committee was set up in 1985 with Shri G. V.K. Rao to review the administrative arrangements for rural development. In that connection it was recommended that Zilla Parishad should be the principal agency to manage all development works at the district level through a number of sub-committees elected on the basis of proportional representation.

The Sarkaria Commission in its Report on Centre-State relations also commented on some aspects of decentralised planning. It focussed on the need for participation of people's representative on the planning and administrative machinery at the local level. It also recommended the creation of a body akin to the Finance Commission at the State level for devolution or transfer of resources to the districts on an operational and objective basis. This very recommendation later on found expression in the Seventy Third and the Seventy Fourth Amendment of the Constitution. Article 243I and Article 243Y provided for the setting up of State Finance Commission.

Around the same time when (the Seventy Second) Amendment Bill 1991-later on enacted as the Constitution (Seventy third) Amendment Act, 1992- was conceived and drafted, the Planning Commission set up a Committee on Micro-level Planning and involvement of people at Grass root level in February, 1992 following the decisions of the 43rd National Development Council held on 23-24 December, 1991. This was an independent exercise even during the process of Constitutional Amendment on aspects of Micro-planning with the following points:

(a) To define the scope and content of micro level or sub-state level planning in the context of State planning;

(b) To delineate the procedure and to devise steps for making micro-level planning operationally effective and viable; and

(c) To suggest rational and pragmatic ways for involvement of people at grass-root level.

The Committee after thread bare discussions submitted its Report in April, 1993- a period when the 73rd Amendment of the Constitution has already been passed. In that sense there was little scope to follow up the recommendations of the NDC committee once the Constitutional Amendment has taken place. However, since the Committee was set up before the Constitutional Amendment, it would be only reasonable and proper to include this Report under this historical perspective to cover all initiatives before the 73rd Amendment. The salient features of the recommendations are mentioned below:

- Monitoring and evaluation of the micro-level schemes have to be done by the micro-level body.
- Centrally Sponsored Scheme on strengthening of planning machineries may be revised to include technical staff up to the block or the taluka level with cost sharing basis between the Central and State governments.
- Pooling of resources of all institutions to meet training requirements.
- Decentralisation of authority and funds are not enough; there has to be consensus to that. No scope for parallel implementation through competing agencies to create situations of potential conflict.
- Planning Commission need to have fresh look at the adequacy of DISNIC-PLAN Programme.
- Integration of inter-dependent activities within the same sector falling in the domain of micro-planning body has to be the responsibility of the micro planning body.
- Work opportunities for large mass of unemployed and unemployed have to be the exclusive preserve of micro-planning.

- All programmes such as JRY, IRDP, DDP, MNP and local development works be entrusted to micro-planning body.
- All the subjects enumerated in the Eleventh Schedule be brought within the scope of micro-planning.
- Satisfactory planning machinery is to be put in place for effective decentralisation of planning.
- Since the Panchayat institutions are to be adopted for micro-level planning framework, bodies like DRDA, DPB should be merged with the corresponding Panchayat institutions at the district level.
- A concept of incentive outlay be introduced, like that of Gujarat, to foster people's involvement in the planning process and micro-planning.
- Five per cent of State plan outlay be given as untied funds to district and lower levels to be utilised at their sole discretion.
- A minimum of 5 per cent of the total plan outlay of the state be contributed as share of the state to micro-planning body towards Minimum Needs Programme.
- At least one percent of State's Annual Plan outlay should be kept for poverty alleviation and employment generation and placed at the disposal of the village Panchayat.
- Addition to the above, at least 30 percent of the State's Plan outlay should be transferred to sub state level planning bodies for expenditure assigned to them.
- A separate budget accounting head be provided for identifying flow of funds to sub-state level bodies.
- The choice of items on twenty nine items to be entrusted to micro-level planning should be left to the discretion of the concerned State Government.
- Non-government organisations may be associated to provide technical expertise to the micro planning body in areas of public health, literacy campaign, environmental issues, alternative and renewable sources of energy etc.
- Knowledge people like school teachers, college teachers, progressive farmers, social workers, professional people

etc., may be associated for the exercise of decentralised planning.

- Formation of Village Development Committees for overseeing implementation of schemes be explored.
- Youths be involved for the creation of community assets through 'Shram Dan'.
- Fair trial to the Gujarat Government concept of 'Sarvodya Yojana' be given.
- Hill states may work out their own arrangement for operationalising the concept of micro-planning.

An overview of the historical perspective on decentralisation initiatives up to the pre-Constitutional Amendment period indicated national faith and collective conviction on the meritorious role of Panchayats as platform for rural development and that several experimentations on Panchayats were tried out based on evolving scenario in the rural areas. The historical account also captures the sequence of search on various options and formulations to find out the right model for decentralised rural governance for the country. Interestingly, the search options for right model appeared to be gradually maturing with passage of time and experiences from a simple concept of agency function to an institutional concept of governance. The right institutional model needs to contain at least the following properties:

(a) Panchayats to serve as institutions of Local Self Government

(b) Panchayats to have distinct functional tiers

(c) Elective representatives to run Panchayats for a term

(d) Devolution of functions for each tier of Panchayat

(e) Funds to be placed to the Panchayats for such devolved responsibilities.

The New Era of Constitutional Decentralisation

Against the historical background as above, the Constitution (the Seventy- Second) Amendment Bill, 1991 was enacted as the Constitution (Seventy Third Amendment) Act,

1992 and similarly, the Constitution (Seventy Third Amendment) Bill, 199I was enacted as the Constitution (Seventy Fourth Amendment) Act, 1992.

The historical perspectives were elaborately captured in the Statement of Objects and Reasons for the introduction of the Bills. From planning focus, the Statement mentioned that the Panchayats have not been able to acquire the status and dignity of viable and responsive people's body due to a number of reasons including inadequate devolution of powers and financial resources. Similarly, the urban local bodies are not able to perform effectively as vibrant democratic units of self government for inadequate devolution of powers and functions. Accordingly, the purpose of Constitutional Amendment for the Panchayats, from planning angle, has been, among other things, devolution by the State legislature of powers and responsibilities upon the Panchayats for preparation of plans for economic development and social justice for the implementation of development schemes. Similarly the purpose for the Constitutional Amendments for the Municipalities, from planning angle, has been preparation of plans for economic development and social justice, and for the implementation of development schemes as may be required to enable them to function as institutions of self-government.

Article 243G enumerates the characteristics and function of new generation of Panchayats as below:

243G. Powers, authority and responsibilities of Panchayat.

Subject to the provisions of the Constitution the Legislature of a State may, by law, endow the Panchayats with such powers and authority as may be necessary to enable them as institutions of self-government and such law may contain provisions for devolution of powers and responsibilities upon Panchayats, at the appropriate level, subject to such condition as may be specified therein, with respect to-

(a) the preparation of plans for economic development and social justice;

(b) the implementation of schemes for economic development and social justice as may be entrusted to them including those in relation to the matters listed in the Eleventh Schedule

The salient features of the above mentioned Article are the following:

(i) Concerned State Legislature to enact legislation on Panchayat.

(ii) Such Panchayats are to function as institutions of self-government.

(iii) Devolution of powers and responsibilities need to take place separately for each of the tiers of Panchayats.

(iv) Empowerment of planning authority for economic development and social justice with respect to devolved functions has to be institutionalised.

(v) Implementation authority both for devolved and assigned schemes are also to be provided.

Similarly, Article 243W enumerates the characteristics and function of new generation of Municipalities as below:

243W. Powers, authority and responsibilities of Municipalities, etc.-

Subject to the provisions of the Constitution the Legislature of a State may, by law, endow –

(a) the Municipalities with such powers and authority as may be necessary to enable them as institutions of self-government and such law may contain provisions for devolution of powers and responsibilities upon Municipalities, subject to such condition as may be specified therein, with respect to-

(c) the preparation of plans for economic development and social justice;

(d) the performance of functions and the implementation of schemes as may be entrusted to them including those in relation to the matters listed in the Twelfth Schedule.

The salient features of the above mentioned Article are the following:

(i) Concerned State Legislature to enact legislation on Municipalities.

(ii) Such Municipalities are to function as institutions of self-government.

(iii) Devolution of powers and responsibilities has to take place for the Municipalities.

(iv) Authority for planning for economic development and social justice with respect to devolved functions has to be given to the Municipalities.

(v) Implementation authority both for devolved and assigned schemes has also to be provided to the Municipalities.

After assigning the planning function to the respective units of three-tier Panchayats for the rural areas and to the Municipalities for the related urban areas, the next logical step arises in combining the said plans into an Integrated Plan for the district. The Constitution makers were alive to the crucial role of consolidation of rural plans and urban plans and accordingly provided for a separate institution, namely, District Planning Committee at the District level. Article 243ZD enumerates the provision for the District Planning Committee as below :

243ZD.Committee for District Planning-

(1) There shall be constituted in every State at the district level a District Planning Committee to consolidate the plans prepared by the Panchayats and the Municipalities in the district and to prepare a draft development plan for the district as a whole.

(2) The Legislature of a State may, by law, make provision with respect to-

(a) the composition of the District Planning Committee;

(b) the manner in which the seats in such Committees shall be filled:

provided that not less than four-fifths of the total number of members of such Committee shall be elected by, and from amongst, the elected members of the Panchayat at the district in proportion to the ratio between the population in rural areas and of the urban areas in the district;

(c) the functions relating to district planning which may be assigned to such Committees;

(d) the manner in which the Chairpersons of such Committees be chosen

(3) Every District Planning Committee shall, in preparing the draft development plan,-

(a) have regard to –

(i) matters of common interest between the Panchayats and the Municipalities including spatial planning, sharing of water and other physical and natural resources, the integrated development of infrastructure and environmental conservation;

(ii) the extent and type of available resources whether financial or otherwise;

(b) consult such institutions and organizations as the Governor may, by order, specify.

(4) The Chairperson of every District Planning Committee shall forward the development plan, as recommended by such Committee, to the Government of the State.

The salient features of the Article 243ZD on District Planning Committee (DPC) are the following:

(i) the DPC is to consolidate plans prepared by the Panchayats and the Municipalities and prepare a draft development plan

(ii) The composition of the DPC has to be in the ratio of 80:20 for elected and nominated members; the elected members have to be from the District Panchayat and the Municipalities and their ratio would be in proportion to rural and urban population.

(iii) Draft development plan to look into common interest areas including spatial planning, physical and natural resources, infrastructure and environmental conservation.

(iv) Draft District Plan to be based on financial resources.

Even after the coming into being of the DPC Acts in most of the states and the Constitution mandated DPCs also having put in place and started functioning, the quality of the district plans, with notable exceptions, has not reached desirable standard. Such district plans have not turned out to be a good reference on vision, priorities and future shaping programmes. Resources back-up between proposed outlay and its prioritised programmes have not been very encouraging either. Besides, a lot of other systemic problems connected with the functioning of the DPC have surfaced. These problems centre essentially around institutional reforms and need speedier redressal to comply with the very spirit and directions of the Constitution for the decentralised governance in the country.

The Relation between the State Plan and the District Plans

There is variation of understanding on the relation between the State Plan and the District Plans. The popular perception is that the State Plan is the summation of district plans. This symbiotic relationship between the State plan and the District plans is based on existence of an ideal premise where the State Government disaggregates the total plan outlay among its districts on some defined norms and asks the concerned District Planning authority to plan for them. The District Plans, thus emerged, would add up as the State Plan. This ideal premise is, however, hardly available or practicable in real-life situation. As a matter of fact, it is just not possible to have any separate Planning authority at the district level to plan for subjects meant for State Government departments nor is it permissible for any district planning authority to plan for state level projects spanning over a number of districts. Another way of looking at the above premise is that at the end of the day, irrespective of the authority of plan formulations, all plans meant for the districts have necessarily to add up to the total of the State Plan outlay. This is a truism and a very simplistic way of looking on the subject. Besides, it does not factor in planning functions as a premise for hazarding such views. The basic point that remains to be resolved is whether all draft plans prepared at the level of the Constitution mandated District Planning Committees would ultimately add up the State Plan. This is the crucial test and is linked with the niceties of planning and the State Government's constitutional responsibility on State Plan and its budgeting.

The State Plan embodies in general the planning efforts on items included in State List and Concurrent List under the Seventh Schedule of the Constitution. More specifically, it covers items of the Line departments in the State Plan as per notification issued under the Rules of Business of Article 166(3) of the Constitution of India. The District Plan, on the other hand, reflects a consolidated picture of plans prepared by the Panchayats and the Municipalities for devolved items under the Eleventh and the Twelfth Schedule of the Constitution respectively. In other words, the planning responsibilities of the departments of a State Government are different from the planning responsibilities of the tiers of the Panchayat and the Municipalities. Thus, jurisdiction over functional items is important and it finally determines the areas on planning. Incidentally, empowerment on defined subjects on areas of planning has lead to the emergence of planning rights over them in favour of any tier of Panchayats in the rural areas or to any municipality in the urban areas. Such planning rights cannot be delegated or usurped by any other planning authority. It is for the same reason that the DPC cannot abrogate to itself the planning rights either of the Panchayats or the Municipalities nor can it subsume the planning rights of the State Planning department/State Planning Board.

This apart, the planning rights of the Panchayats and the Municipalities pertain to items as devolved on to them. Its jurisdiction on planning items is limited to devolved items only. It does have neither the mandate nor the competency to plan for items included under State List or Concurrent List. It is for the same reason that plans of such rural and urban local bodies, as consolidated into District Plan, need not be looked upon as sub-sets of the State Plan .The planning areas are distinct and different for the State and for each of the tiers of the Panchayats or for the Municipalities.

There is admittedly inherent linkage between schemes of the State plan with schemes of the decentralised plans on development functional area and that interactions within them in a time format would enable them to broaden planning vision and shared perception, refocusing related planning priorities and revisiting its sectoral allocation. In other words, the Planning role of the State is independent of the planning roles at the levels of Panchayats and the Municipalities and vice versa, though there may exist programme and planning connectivity in some areas. The nature, scope and character of State Plan and District Plans are different as per constitutional provision.

Further, the State Plan, in ideal setting, could have been an amalgamation of all items included in the District Plans and also those included in the Plans of the Line departments of the State Government in the districts. However, this ideal setting is missing in almost all the States and such amalgamation is not possible for other valid reasons also. Unlike resources meant for the State Plan, the District Plans, in most cases, are not prepared on the basis of firm resources. Further, own resources of the Panchayats and the Municipalities, however big or small as it may be, happen to be very significant components of resources for local level planning. Such resources are not taken into consideration for computing resources meant for the State Plan. Additionally, in absence of real devolution in most states, the items in the District Plans also include projected fund for assigned schemes in favour of the Panchayats or the Municipalities, which incidentally have already been booked by the concerned plan implementing departments in their departmental State Annual Plan. There is real danger of double counting on this crucial area. On top of it all, there is no provision in the Constitution of India requiring the Planning Commission either to approve or to disapprove of District Plans and, therefore, incorporation of such District Plans within State Plan would amount to seeking Planning Commission's approval in a round about way which it is not permissible under the Constitutional mandate. The State Plan, in real terms, is the aggregation of the plans of the Line departments only. The Planning Commission approves this aggregated State Plan, presented under major or minor heads of development, after due process of assessment of state resources, Working Group discussions in the Planning Commission with the secretaries of the Line departments and finally after Deputy Chairman-Chief Minister level of interactions. The State Plan, as approved by the Planning Commission, is also required to be approved by the State Cabinet before taking it up for budgeting by the State. The State Plan becomes functional from the next financial year after it is so budgeted.

The District Plans in the Constitutional scheme of things on the other hand are, required to be sent to the State Government as per Article 243ZD(4) ibid. Such District Plan comes back to the concerned District Planning Committee with State Government's comments, if any. There is no scope to accord cabinet approval or approval by any department of state government on such District Plans. There is also no scope to follow up the budgeting exercise either by the State Government or by the DPC. The responsibility of budgeting its Annual Plan lies with the related unit of the tier of Panchayats as provided under the State Panchayat Act or with the Municipalities under the State Municipal Act. The District Planning Committee is required only to send back the State Government's observations, if any, on the draft Annual Plan to all units of Panchayats and Municipalities for appropriate action. The respective local bodies, after due consideration of such observations, then approve its plan and take measures to budget for them. The procedural format for plan approval and its budgeting is also different for each tier of the Panchayat or the Municipalities. It is an independent function not connected in any way with the State Plan. In the circumstances, it would not be fair to hold that

State Plan is an aggregated version of District Plans of any State. The District Plans are in fact by its own nature functionally different and in no way qualify to be sub-sets of the State Plan.

Conceptial Clarifications on Related Issues on Planning

(a) Planning, Plan and Plan of Action

Uniformity of understanding is not the hallmark of decentralised planning in our country. It is usually plagued by plural perceptions originating from three linked concepts, namely (i) Planning, (ii) Plan and (iii) Plan of Action. These concepts are mutually exclusive and are not substitutable one for the other. As a matter of fact, liberal use of these concepts to convey the same kind of meaning has distracted the focus on decentralised planning. It is, therefore, a necessity that these concepts be briefly addressed for role clarification to facilitate proper district planning in our country:

(i) Planning

Planning is a process in which vision is settled; objectives are outlined with due regard to human development deficit; felt needs of the stake holders are assessed by direct interaction or otherwise; stocktaking of resources, both physical, financial and human are made; prioritisation is decided after examining all possible alternatives and then final decision is made on schemes, its location and its financial provisioning. The issues of inclusiveness, bridging the divide, targeting the BPL, SC, ST, children, women and the aged fall in the domain of planning.

(ii) Plan

Plan is the document in which the final decisions on planning are captured. The document could be simple; it can also be detailed depending on requirement to present the Plan e.g. the presentation of Annual Plan of a State to the Planning Commission has to be made in 15 annexure. However, there are some common characters for presentation of any Plan like the name of the planning authority, the nature of plan-Annual/

Revised, the planning year, sector wise presentation of schemes along with proposed outlay etc. It may also include physical targets, separate provisioning for SC/ST/Women/NGOs, etc.

District Plans of the country right at this point of time do not have any designed format but need to have a common presentation format just as all the tiers of the Panchayats and the Municipalities should have also structured format for presentation of Plans. Any format with built-in planning concepts not only introduces discipline and logic in the presentation of Plan, it also takes care of confusion prevailing in the area, besides facilitating proper consolidation of plans at the level of the District Planning Committee. It will also enable to make intra and inter district comparison of plan initiatives based on objective reality. This is a big reform area in decentralised planning in our country.

(iii) Plan of Action

Plan of Action comes into the picture after the Plan of any local body is finalised. This is a function relating to execution of schemes of those approved in the Plan. Plan of action is in fact a third layer of activity and is not directly connected with the process of planning, a first layer of activity which has already been over. It has only connectivity with schemes included in the Plan for follow-up action. This is true for all approved schemes in a Plan irrespective of whether it is a devolved scheme or any assigned scheme. There is no scope for *de novo* planning at this stage of way forward. The focused responsibility at this stage is only to work out action points for execution of schemes, popularly known as Plan of Action.

The Plan of Action has assumed importance with the coming into being of NAREGA, BRGF, RKVY, etc. Since such schemes have tied-up big resources which in a way determine the spending image of the related local body, separate planning and Plan of Action have come as conditionalties for eligibility of fund under such schemes. These new dimensions have complicated the area of planning.

Planning is a time bound job of a tier of Panchayats or Municipalities for its Annual Plan. There is normally no scope for parallel planning for each of assigned schemes separately at different points of time. However, when a local body accepts any assigned scheme, it will have no option but to agree to the conditionality of parallel planning and submit Plan of Action .In that event, it may or may not correspond with the timelines of its Annual Plan. In any case, it is desirable to present such assigned schemes separately under caption 'assigned scheme' in the plan presentation format itself. It will never form a part of the basic plan of local body which is meant for devolved schemes only. Plan of Action for each of the schemes including assigned schemes may be worked out separately, shared with assignee and executed.

(b) Devolution vs Assigned Schemes

The meaning of devolution, as earlier explained, has three essential components namely, autonomy in respect of selection of scheme, its financial provisioning and also of its implementation. That is to say, the concerned local body is sovereign in respect of devolved schemes and it need not refer to the government functionary for its approval or fund. The Constitution of India requires institutional devolution to put in place by the Legislature of a State, under Article 243G, on items of the Eleventh Schedule to each of the tiers of the Panchayat and also on items of the Twelfth Schedule to the Municipalities as per Article 243W.

Assigned schemes are those entrusted to any tier of the Panchayats or to the Municipalities either by the departments of the State Government or by the Ministries of the Central Government under defined terms and conditions. The terms and conditions may be rigid; it can be very flexible also. Unlike devolved responsibilities, it is not a kind of institutional empowerment by the Legislature of a State on functional items under the Eleventh Schedule to each tier of the Panchayat or to the Municipalities on items of the Twelfth Schedule. It is scheme specific and not functional responsibility specific. Assigned schemes are also not permanent in nature but valid for the term of assignment. Such assignment may be revoked by the assignee at any time on ground of exigency of the government. Here the role of the local body is akin to the role of an agency and that it has also to comply with all the conditionalities and directions of its assignee. It has in that sense less sovereign power over the scheme and is liable to be controlled by the assignee or its representatives. Assigned schemes are thus not devolved schemes as they do not meet the devolution criteria.

It is in this context that the role of devolved schemes and the role of assigned schemes on Annual Plan assumes importance and need comprehensive resolution. Article 243G and Article 243W have empowered respectively the levels of Panchayats and the Municipalities to plan for devolved items; it has not mentioned anything about assigned schemes. This is for the simple reason that while assignment is a task concept, devolution is a right concept. The Constitution of India did not envisage master-servant relationship in between the State Government and the Local Self Governments and accordingly desired to empower these Local Governments with devolution of functions under constitutional protection. Assignment of schemes or functions cannot be substitute for devolution and need not be equated with devolution. Incidentally, Kerala, the front ranking State in the country on decentralisation has used the word assignment of functions (Appendices 2.2) and it is only desirable that sooner the word assignment of functions is replaced with devolution of functions it is better for the way forward towards devolution. Therefore, for ensuring purity in the planning arena, the levels of the Panchayat and the Municipalities need to focus on planning for devolved schemes only. However, having regard to the fact that there has not taken place proper devolution across the states of India, except Kerala, and also having taken into consideration that assigned schemes need not pass as proxy indicator for devolution, there is necessity to have a separate segment in the format for Annual Plan presentation to capture plan proposals for assigned schemes. This would enable to compare the planning character of both the options.

(C) Plan and Non-Plan Items

The conceptual clarity on classification of Plan and Non-Plan activities is very important from planning point of view. Any new scheme taken up in any Annual Plan or under a Five Year Plan belongs to the category of Plan Scheme. The salient feature of a plan scheme is that it has an outcome content connected with the basic objective and goal of an Annual Plan or under a Five Year Plan. The nature of such outcome may be different depending on whether such scheme belongs to Primary sector. Secondary sector or Tertiatory sector. Non-plan items, on the other hand, falls in the category of maintenance of those schemes which were completed earliers. It is a kind of committed liability under Non-plan. However, upgradation of a previously completed scheme falls under Plan scheme. Additionally, organizational expenses including contingencies related expenditures fall under Non-plan. For the same reason, Non-plan items do not qualify to be included under Plan. This classification for the State plan is maintained under the watchful eyes of the Accounted General in the state. This clarification, ipso factor, is also applicable for the Panchayat and the Municipality also it is fundamental in nature.

(d) The Line Department in the District and its Role in the District Plan

There exists perceptional variations on the role of the line Department of the Government working in the district and their relation in the District Plan. The District Plan, under Article 243ZD, is a consolidation outcome of Plans prepared by the Panchayats and the Municipalities, Legally speaking, there is no scope for the Plans of the Line Departments of the State Government to be part of such District Plan. On the basis of devolved functional items out of the 11th Schedule under Article 243G or out of the 12th Schedule under Article 243W, the Panchayats and the Municipalities have been empowered to plan on them and then submit it to the DPC. The state of imperfect devolution coupled with assignment of the agency functions of the departments of the state government/Central government to the tiers of the Panchayats and the Municipalities has made the planning area rather confusing and complicated. Non-devolved items along with some assigned schemes of the government departments have forced their presence in the plan of the Panchayats on the Municipalities. As per Rules of Bussiness, Under Article 166(3) of the Constitution of India, the Line-department of the government are to plan and implement schemes as are covered under List II and List III of the Seventh Schedule and such works are executed in the district of the state. The exclusion of Planning efforts of such line departments in any districts make the District Plan less wholesome. From planning angle, those planning efforts are needed to be captured and made part of the District Plan. This is a critical area of reforms under the District Plan and needs to be addressed early.

2

Role of the District Planning Committee in District Planning and in the District Plan

The Seventy Third and Seventy Fourth Amendments of the Constitution of India ushered a new regime of decentralised planning in our country. The top-down approach to planning has given way to bottom-up planning under a constitutional mandate. In working out this grassroots planning, the Constitution has given appropriate consideration to capture the voices and opinions of the citizens of the given locality. The Gram Sabha in the rural areas and the Ward Sabha in the urban areas are expected to serve as outposts of sensors of citizens' felt-need and priorities of the locality. The three-tier of Panchayats in the rural areas and Municipalities in the urban areas have been empowered to formulate plans based on local level priorities under the expressed provisions of the Constitution. All of such local bodies are now local government institutions in our country and have been vested with planning function of their given responsibilities. The plans prepared by the three tier Panchayats would form the rural plan and the plans prepared by the Municipalities would form the urban plan of the district. The job of the District Planning Committee is to consolidate plans prepared by the Panchayats and the Municipalities and prepare the draft development of the district. For the said reason, the District Planning Committees have come into being in almost all the states of India as a compliance of the mandatory provision of Article 243ZD.

The District Planning Committee is the apex planning body at the district level invested with enormous responsibility to guide the decentralised planning bodies to formulate their own plans based on objective realities and ensure adequate interaction and participation with the citizens. The preparation of resource based plans, its prioritisation and compliance with time lines are areas in which the DPC is required to give appropriate guidance. The responsibility of all administrative and procedure related guidance, in so far it relates to consolidation of draft development plan, falls on the DPC also. However, it cannot directly interfere with the discharge of the planning function of such local bodies. Since the responsibility of the DPC is limited to consolidation in the District Plan of aggregated plan outlay already decided at the levels of Panchayats and the Municipalities, the scope for further planning by the DPC for areas of such local self Government is not permissible. For the same reason, the Constitution of India has not empowered the DPC with independent and parallel planning function. However, as the apex constitutional planning body in the district, it has the authority to request such levels of Panchayats and the Municipalities to reconsider plan priorities and investment decisions, if deemed necessary. Once such reconsidered decisions are made available to the DPC, the process of consolidation commences on.

The function of the DPC is consolidation of plans prepared by the Panchayats and the Municipalities. In so doing, the Constitution of India has required the DPC to keep in the upfront matters of common interest between the Panchayats and

Municipalities. The DPC is also to ensure that spatial planning related issues, sharing of water and other physical and natural resources may not create any conflict of interest among the tiers of Panchayats, among the Municipalities or among the Panchayats and the Municipalities and disturb the planning process. In this respect, the Constitution has given due authority to the DPC in the enabling provision of Article 243ZD to resolve the matter. Further, development of infrastructure in a district depends on conscious efforts of all planning authorities to work together in close cooperation, in spirit of harmony and also in discharging shared responsibility. The spirit of partnership should be the driving force for owning this task. The DPC has constitutional responsibility to put in place such collective and unifying approach and ensure that micro-level planning is not to serve a closed and narrow geographical limit alone but is also open-ended to interlink with the planning process of other programme partners in the district and serve the greater interest by its own contribution to a shared goal.

Similarly, environmental conservation is not a onetime affair nor it is the sole responsibility of any particular local government. Conservation is a process of sustained efforts over time and it is more so for environmental conservatism. It is the responsibility of all citizens, all local governments, all state and national governments and beyond as environment is a local issue, it is a state issue, it is a national issue and it is also a global issue. The responsibility is joint and several. It is the responsibility of all local governments to keep environmental conversation issue in the centrality of its planning efforts, in the implementation of its programme efforts and also in all its regulatory efforts. It is to be looked into by the DPC that all plan proposals from the Panchayats and the Municipalities in the district need to conform to environmental compatibility before taking up consolidation function for the draft district plan.

Additionally, it is also Constitutional responsibility for the DPC to ensure that the plan proposals of all local bodies have been duly incorporated after taking into consideration the extent and type of resources, whether financial or otherwise. It is often found that in their zeal to project a better image, a good number of schemes are often included by local bodies under their plan proposals with no identified resources in sight. Such notional schemes are unqualified to come under any Annual Plan proposals for any local body. Similarly, proposals for schemes based on inadequate or notional resources are also not qualified to come under any decentralised plan. All of such plan proposals have to be returned to the concerned local body for appropriate follow-up.

Furthermore, as mentioned earlier, the State Plan is not a summation of all district plans on grounds of different role functions in the given planning architecture. The areas of difference between the State Plan and the District Plan are also due to financial resources surrounding the State Plan and the District Plan. The State Government prepares the Annual Plan based on availability of identified plan resources as agreed by the Planning Commission. Non-plan fund are booked separately by the State for the Annual Non-plan budget. In the case of Panchayats or the Municipalities, the system of separate Annual Plan and separate Annual Non-plan has yet to come in vogue for a good many valid reasons. The culture of accounting system, the quality of accounts-men at their disposal, the non-availability of the award of the State Finance Commission separately for Plan and Non-plan items in favour of either the Panchayats or the Municipalities are some of the factors that do not favour the growth of Plan and Non-plan specific institutional knowledge, its management or its provisioning in the budget. Additionally, even after the Constitutional Amendment, the State Non-plan head continues to provide grant-in aid for the Panchayats and the Municipalities unconnected with the recommendations of the State Finance Commission. The upshot of the discussion is that the possibility of inclusion of Non-plan items of development expenditure in the Draft Development Plan is very real. Moreover, in absence of a clear-cut guideline on Plan and Non-plan items of expenditure for specified items covered under the Eleventh schedule or the Twelfth schedule, the Panchayats or the Municipalities very often include Non-plan nature of development works in the Draft Development Plan within items devolved on to them. If the scheme of financing of a local body' plan includes Non-plan type of developmental expenditure also, there is every chance for it to escape the scrutiny layer and join unintentionally in the consolidation process which needs to be appropriately guarded. The DPC has to look after this critical area of confusion and need also to issue formal guidelines.

Another area that calls for extreme caution is with respect to schemes being taken up under Annual Plan by the line departments in the districts. As a general practice, the line departments of the State Government implement both the state sector schemes as well as district sector schemes subsequent to allocation of responsibilities under the Rules of Business of the State under Article166(3). In such States where devolution has taken place after very detailed functional mapping on areas of common functional jurisdiction between the departments of the state government vis-a-vis the local bodies, the line departments of the State would have clear and well defined functions. In other situations, there would exist overlapping jurisdiction between the line departments of the State and its local bodies, rural or urban. However, in both situations, the line departments of the State would also be implementing district sector schemes and would have corresponding departmental district plan. Given the constitutional directives under Article 243ZD, the DPC can only take into consideration of plans prepared by the Panchayats and Municipalities and not district plans of such line departments. This is an interesting void area in the District Plan. For complete coverage plan schemes in a district, it is indeed desirable to include such departmental plan schemes in the district under the District Plan. It would then give complete picture of district plan schemes in a particular year and make it easier to work on productive coordination and convergence in between schemes of the Panchayats/Municipalities with schemes of the line departments, whereever possible, right from its planning stage. This is a felt-need reform area in the jurisdiction of the DPC. Be that as it may, given the position as it exists, the DPC need to organise a supplementary of departmental plans (location wise, if possible) in the district and append it with its draft development plan for appropriate use by the rural and urban local bodies in the district till such time as the Constitutional amendment takes place.

Similarly, plans prepared by the NGOS in the district also remain unconnected with Draft District Plan. Based on the National Policy on Voluntary Sectors, the Civil Society organisations and the NGOs have been working in different sectors both in the rural and in urban areas. These organisations address works usually in the same common area of the Panchayats or the Municipalities and have their own work plan with virtually no connection with mainstream local bodies' plan in the district .Such organisations receive funds from various sources including the Central Government and the State Government. The annual plans of such organisations are usually not informed either to the concerned local body having the territorial jurisdiction or to the DPC. This is a grey area of duplication of efforts. For prevention of such duplication and wastage of crucial human and financial resources, a mechanism needs to be built up at the planning stage of such NGOs to ensure that it does not stray in the devolved functional areas of the Panchayats or the Municipalities. This is an area where the DPC may intervene and require all voluntary sectors to submit their Annual Plans (location wise, if possible) and append them with the draft district plan for transparency and appropriate follow-up, where ever required.

Credit Plans of the Financial Institutions are outside the planning responsibility of the DPC. The empowered responsibility for the Credit Plan falls on the financial institutions with Lead bank in the district as its coordinator and the District Level

Bankers' Committee (DLBC) as the final deciding authority. Banks and other financial institutions are partners in promoting development programmes in the district like the Government departments, the Panchayats and the Municipalities. They assist the customer-citizens in two ways: by meeting credit component of government sponsored schemes and also by way of meeting diverse credit needs out of banks' own portfolio of schemes. However, the credit plan of financial institutions is not prepared at the local branch level. In this sense it is not decentralised in character. It is prepared at higher level and communicated to the local branch unit. Incidentally, there is no connectivity between the planning process of the local bodies and the credit planning process of the banks. The timelines for credit plan are also different from local bodies' timelines for preparation of plans. Besides, in absence of clear devolution of functional jurisdiction, the scope for indication of credit-linked schemes and number of its possible beneficiaries is also not straight forward. Even then based on ongoing credit-linked schemes in the area, the concerned local body may assist the related banks in the area / DLBC by way of informing possible beneficiaries. Such limited input might even be useful to work on supply side of the credit need. In course of time the process would get itself fine-tuned with the given system and make the credit plan more earthly and real .Micro-level supportive credit plan for the related annual plan of the related local body may emerge. The DPC would be in a position to interact once the draft District Credit plan is ready and ask the DLBC to revisit the identified areas.

The DPC and the Check-lists for Consolidation

For preparing the draft district plan, the DPC is required to consolidate plans prepared by the tiers of Panchayats and Municipalities. In performing its consolidation function smoothly, it would be useful to have a standard check list for scrutiny on draft plans submitted by the tiers of Panchayats and Municipalities. A model of such checklist is given below:

(a) Planning for Respective Devolved Items

The Constitution of India requires the State legislature under Article 243G to devolve distinct functional items of the Eleventh Schedule on each of the tiers of Panchayat in the State. Similarly, it requires functional items of the Twelfth Schedule to be devolved on to the Municipalities under Article 243W. On the basis of decision on such devolved items, the concerned local body is entitled to undertake planning exercise for the Five Year Plan/Annual Plan. In the event any State Government has not devolved such items formally, such local bodies are not eligible to plan for them. It is a necessary condition for enabling the local bodies to plan for them. The sufficient condition is that such devolution has to be tier specific and there shall not exist any confusion about planning jurisdiction on devolved subjects. It is now to be looked into by the DPC whether the concerned local bodies have duly worked on such devolved items and made plan on them.

(b) Planning for Assigned Scheme Schemes, if any

Generally speaking, the intention of the Constitution of India has been on devolution to enable them to grow as institutions of local government. It did not visualise that such institutions would be utilised primarily as implementing agents for programmes of the State Government or Central Government. Be that as it may, Gram Panchayats, Block Panchayats or Zilla Panchayat or Municipalities are now very often assigned to execute certain national or state schemes. Implementation of such schemes needs to be preceded by working out detailed planning for them. Some such schemes also fall in the category of Flagship Programme of the country, namely, NAREGA or JNNURM, etc. Some other important schemes assigned to them include BRGF (Backward Scheme Grant Fund), RSVY (Rashtriya Sam Vikash Yojana), JSY (Janani Suraksha Yojana) etc. The funds in question of all such schemes are made available to local bodies for planning and execution of schemes by the Central Government through the State

Government. The DPC may also scrutinise whether such schemes have been incorporated under their respective plan and included as plan resources.

(c) Compliance with Statutory Provisions, if Any

Apart from the devolved items, the relevant State Act may have invested power and authority in respect of certain traditional functions which hitherto belonged to the concerned rural or urban body. Such functions might as well be connected in a very broad sense with items under the Eleventh Schedule or the Twelfth Schedule. In case such functions do have components for planning, the DPC has to see that it has been so captured in the proposed plans of such local bodies.

(d) The Observance of Planning Process

Planning process is as important as the Plan itself. As a matter of fact, the strength of the decentralised planning lies in accommodating felt needs of local people and also in their participation in the planning process of prioritisation and selection of schemes. The quality of the plan depends to a large extent on quality of planning process. The importance of the planning process can be understood from the fact that the Constitution of India itself provided forum of Gram Sabha in the rural areas and Ward Sabha for the Municipalities for consultations and sensoring public perception on priorities. This apart, the Planning Commission, the State Government and the DPC also issue guidelines on the virtue of consultation with stake holders as important part of the planning process. It would, therefore, require the DPC to see whether the Plan so prepared by the concerned local body has been formally sent after holding prior interactions and consultations with Gram Sabha/ Ward Sabha, as the case may be, within the overall guidelines issued in this regard.

(e) Resources Back-up for Plan Proposals

No plan is meaningful and implementable unless it is backed up by matching fund. The culture of resource-based planning is not the hallmark of decentralised local bodies in any state. As a matter of fact, it has yet to take deep root as a part of discipline and culture at the decentralised level. It is very often found that the plan of a local body ultimately turns out to be a mere wish-list of schemes or a catalogue of schemes and serves to please all. However, planning is a serious subject of prioritisation based on identified resources, and schemes so prioritised in the plan are meant for implementation only. In other words, there has to exist one to one correspondence between availability of fund and the schemes included in the Plan. The DPC has, therefore, to look into resource-back up, both tied and untied, for the Annual Plan submitted by the concerned local body. Since such scrutiny has to take place before the process of consolidation takes place, it would be advisable for such local bodies to attach a resource back-up sheet (i.e. the scheme of financing the Plan) along with plan proposals. The process of consolidation commences after the scrutiny is over.

(f) Adherence to Stipulated Environmental and Other Norms

The plan proposals of the decentralised local bodies are often linked with environmental issues and its possible impact on environmental conservatism. It is to be looked into by the DPC whether centrality of environmental conservation issues are embedded in all plan proposals of the Panchayats and the Municipalities and that such proposals do conform to environmental compatibility before taking up consolidation function for the draft district plan.

(g) Format for Plan Presentation

Format is an essential requirement for presentation of any Plan. Unless the Plans are presented in any uniform format either by the tiers of the Panchayat or by the Municipalities, it would not permit to find out the features of either the Rural Plan or Urban Plan of the district. It would also not permit to consolidate plans prepared by the Panchayats and the Municipalities and then prepare the draft development plan of the District. A necessary condition is that the decentralised plans have to be prepared on the basis of uniform development functional concepts and also present it at a consolidation friendly given format.

3

Planning Issues of Decentralised Planning

Governance issues and planning issues are often used in the same breadth at the decentralised level creating a lot of confusion at the planning area. Governance issues are in fact interwoven with governance functions itself and more particularly with the quality of good governance functions. It covers issues of authority, accountability, stewardship, leadership, and direction and control exercised in the organisation. The good governance on the other hand denotes the organisation's ability to function credibly, to achieve its objectives and complying with all the legal, ethical and operational requirements of an organisation.

Based on hundreds of specific and disaggregated individual variables measuring various dimensions of governance, the World Bank designed World wide Governance Indicators (WGI) which reflects the relative performance of countries in respect of six indicators namely:

- Voice and accountability
- Political stability
- Government effectiveness

- Regulatory quality
- Rule of law
- Control of corruption

The fundamentals of these issues are also applicable to all institutions including the levels of Panchayats and Municipalities.

Planning issues at the decentralised level, on the other hand, are connected with nature of devolved items, its current status, citizens' perception on priorities, identifying development deficit, possible alternative options for improvement on infrastructure, livelihood, health, education, etc. Inclusiveness and bridging the divide also fall on the planning issues. However, there is a linkage between governance issues and planning issues in that the governance issues ultimately determine the quality of performance of items planned and good planning also helps to ensure good governance. In other words, good governance is a necessary condition for realisation of planning objectives.

Planning issues at the decentralised level, unlike state plan, are more down to earth. Here connectivity with the people is more open, direct and linked with expectation. Therefore, irrespective of planning objectives of the national or state plan, two aspects dominate the planning expectation at the decentralised level:

(i) Plan must address objective reality to improve quality of life

(ii) It needs to show demonstrable results at the quickest point of time.

Based on the above two expectations, all related planning activities revolve around - objectives, formulation of schemes, its implementation and monitoring. However, these are not very simple as it may appear. The understanding of perception of felt needs and objective reality are as diverse as the plural number of heads in the given area. The consensus building exercise, however, enables the people to own the plan as their own. Central to the said consensus building is the items to be selected for planning and its prioritisation. The intended outcome is overall agreement on people's perception on felt needs vis-à-vis the options available under devolved items for the local body. Other issues relevant in such interactions include current status on human development deficit, general perception of prioritisation, inclusive growth issues and the current status of quality of implementation of ongoing schemes including assigned schemes (e.g. NAREGA). This forum serves as a platform for sensoring public perception and consultation for taking pragmatic decision on Annual Plan of the local body. Needless to mention, it is not the forum for final decision on planning priorities; the final decision would be taken by the concerned local body in its statutory meeting based on inputs received through interactions and other materials.

Planning issues at the decentralised level are both collective as well as domain specific. It is a shared responsibility for all programme partners to meet the mighty challenge of development in the district under the leadership of the DPC. Incidentally, the role and scope of the decentralised planning bodies is different from those of the line departments in the district or other partners. The planning exercises would also tend to vary within the district itself based on the functional limits of the decentralised bodies-rural or urban, and in case of rural areas, it will vary with respective level (tier) of Panchayats. Incidentally, decentralised plans also tend to vary from one district to another just as any Gram Panchayat Plan, Block Panchayat Plan or a Municipal Plan within a district differs from another on account of ground realities, local priorities, functional limits and differential status on development.

One of the district specific macro issues on planning which need to be addressed collectively is the deficit in human development as revealed in the District Human Development Report. District Development Report, District Education Survey, Health Survey, Nutrition Survey, Drinking Water Survey, etc. also open up gaps and deficit on social and economic achievement and require repositioning planning interventions on actionable areas .The role of the DPC in this area is important.

It would be useful in this context to mention some of the district level macro issues on planning which the decentralised local bodies need to interact jointly but act severely at its jurisdiction level.

National Five Year Plans and Decentralised issues

Planning is a dynamic and continuous process. The planning scenario of the country undergoes generational changes with every five year plan. Accordingly, with every new five year plan comes new approaches, newer objectives and revisiting of priorities with different emphasis on sectoral provisioning. It tends to address emerging planning concern of the time and the related realities. The approval of the new Five Year Plan by the National Development Council gives it a mandate for its implementation for the central government and also for all the state governments. It is also a mandate applicable to all decentralised planning bodies in the country. On closer analysis, however, it will reveal that there are commonalities in the fundamentals of planning across the Five Year Plans. Such commonalities in fundamentals are universal in character and look like grammar of planning, connected as it is with the basic needs of the citizens. From practical angle, it would be of great help if new five year plan related issues are discussed from decentralised focus also and disseminated accordingly. Needless to mention, the planning and implementation responsibility would be both general and several. It is general when similar action is to be taken by all on a planning issue e.g. inclusiveness. It is several when objective decisions are to be taken based on ground reality on a given planning related issue for areas devolved on to them. This is an area where role clarification is extremely important for planning at the decentralised level. It is of utmost importance that each tier of the Panchayat and also each of the Municipalities be informed about the new planning issues of the new Five Year Plan and its linkage with their existing devolution subjects. The discretion of interpretation may not be left on to the individual local body.

Status of BPL

The estimation of poverty, based on whatever method, gives an aggregate picture of the poverty status of the country and also for the States. While such findings do have immense policy implications for the country or for the States, the BPL is the document based on which poverty eradication programmes would have to be actually structured at the micro-level. The BPL is a tool for programme implementation. All rural and urban poverty related programmes in our country are based on targeted programme intervention to bring down the level of poverty. Because of equity attached with the BPL, it is accepted as a high valued document. However, it is not always possible to have a defect-free BPL list because of village politics and murkier role of political parties. As a result, ineligibles very often manage to enjoy subsidized programme benefits at the expense of the very poor, poor and people on the margin. While efforts may be made at the grass roots level to have error-free and validated BPL, the analytical study of the list connected with specific programme is the other important consideration. Further, from operational angle, it is necessary to see that such list does not remain as permanent even after successful execution of related schemes. It needs to be concurrently updated by interactive process based on programme benefits provided by other tier of the Panchayats to those included in the BPL list. The analytical study and its related input is an important consideration while planning at the decentralised level.

District Human Development Report (DHDR)

The Millennium Development Goals (MDGs) are an agreed set of goals that international community set for itself at the UN Millennium Summit 2000. It encompassed universally accepted human values and rights such as freedom from hunger, the right to basic education, the right to health and responsibility to future generations. The MDGs, as set for implementation and monitoring, are as follows:

Goal 1: Eradicate extreme poverty and hunger
Goal 2: Achieve universal primary education
Goal 3: Promote gender equality and empower women
Goal 4: Reduce child mortality
Goal 5: Improve maternal health
Goal 6: Combat HIV/AIDS, malaria and other diseases
Goal 7: Ensure environmental sustainability
Goal 8: Develop a global partnership for development

Sources: UNDP document

The DHDR of a particular edition captures the level of achievements in its HDI and focuses on the need of programme correction to make good of the human development deficit. Improving the DHDR status is the joint and shared responsibility of all programme partners in rural and urban local bodies and requires commensurate response. Planning is an important forum where response is needed for its ultimate outcome. Thus, the issue of varying degree of achievements in Human Development has to be consciously addressed by realistic planning at this level.

Minimum Needs Services

Basic minimum standard of life for all sections of people has been the planning concern of the country since the Fifth Five Year Plan. The Chief Ministers Conference held in July, 1996 endorsed the seven basic minimum services as of paramount importance in securing a better quality of life for the people, especially those residing in rural areas. The seven basic services identified for priority attention are:

- 100 per cent coverage of provision of safe drinking water in rural and urban areas ;
- 100 per cent coverage of primary health service facilities in rural and urban areas ;
- Universalisation of primary education ;
- Provision of Public Housing Assistance to all shelterless poor families ;

- Extension of Mid-day Meal Programme in primary schools, to all rural blocks and urban slums and disadvantaged sections ;
- Provision of connectivity to all unconnected villages and habitations; and
- Streamlining of the Public Distribution System with focus upon the poor.

The essence of focus on this minimum basic services is that though this programme has undergone generational changes both in programme nomenclature, in its content and also in delivery of services, it has all the fundamentals for inclusive plan, tailored as it is with equity issue of human development. These primary areas have to be adequately addressed at the decentralised level.

Infrastructure at the District Level

Infrastructure is the pillar of development and shapes the very foundation of the basic character of the economy. Infrastructure has nation specific, state specific and district specific requirements connected as it is, with basic structure of related sectors at major, medium and minor level. While infrastructure for national economy is concerned with requirement for mega projects having multiplier impact on the economy, the requirement for infrastructure at the state level is to build up foundation for state level projects of different sectors. The infrastructural requirements at the district level are primarily concerned with livelihood and social development. All these infrastructural supports are not mutually exclusive and there exists inherent connectivity among the layers of infrastructure. All of them in aggregate terms determine the infrastructure base of the national economy. Such infrastructural base has also short term, medium term and long term focus and requires upgradation with generational changes in the development scenario.

Based on district vision and the deficit in the current infrastructure status, a blueprint for infrastructural requirement needs to be built up at the level of DPC by the departments of the State government at the district level, the Panchayats at different levels and also by the Municipalities at their own level. While working on infrastructural planning, the decentralised local bodies need to address deficit in infrastructure on Education, Health, Road Connectivity, Sanitation, Housing, Electricity including Village Electrification and Non-conventional Energy Programme, Market Infrastructure, etc. Depending on devolution and also nature of assigned schemes to the local bodies, the funding support for infrastructure could be met from the Bharat Nirman, UDISSIMT, Sarva Siksha Abhyan (SSA), Finance Commission Grant, National Rural Health Mission, ICDS, PMGSY, MGNREGS, RIDF of NABARD, TSC, Indira Awaas Yojana, EWS/LIG Programme, Rajiv Gandhi Grameen Vidyutikaran Yojana, Non-conventional Energy Programme, etc.

Water

Water has emerged as a new focused issue on planning at the decentralisation level. Gone are the days of abundant and relatively comfortable water resources position. The exponential growth of water demand from both traditional and not-so traditional sources has been rapidly turning into a supply constraint scenario. The demand for adequate water as a basic human right has added further dimension . The competitive claim of water by agriculture (India's net irrigated area is still less than 50%), Industries of various descriptions (both water intensive and water based), Power sector (both hydel and thermal), Municipalities and other institutions from Nature's grid of water are bound to increase at a much higher rate. Concurrently at the same time, supply side is being seriously affected by regular shrinkage of catchments in the hills, declining and uneven rainfall status, shrinking carrying capacity of the river beds and reservoirs, warming up of the climate and its consequent impact on lesser volume on surface water reservoirs, over-use of ground water resources, absence of commensurate corrective restoration programmes and its concurrent monitoring, non-recycling of water wastes and the like. The high point on planning on water related issue is making a balance between demand and supply.

The Constitution of India provides authority on Water related areas to the the tiers of Panchayats (item 11 of the 11th Schedule) and to the Municipalities (item 5 of the 12th Schedule) along with the Union Government and the State Government (item 17 of the State List, 7th Schedule). The decentralised local bodies need to address them based on devolution of functional responsibilities among the Panchayats.

While addressing water issues, the decentralised planning bodies, based on its devolution of functions, need also to address (i) Quantity (ii) Accessibility (iii) Quality and (iv) Sustainability aspects, specially in relation to drinking water. The emerging scenario has further enhanced the need for this to be given appropriate consideration:

(i) Shifting of the focus from spot water sources to a regime of micro- piped drinking water supply to serve the dual purpose of quality (arsenic free) of water and inclusive-centred delivery of water services.

(ii) The water supply sources- both surface and ground water- are dynamic in character and calls for periodical verification. GIS based water table maps need to be periodically published for appropriate programme correction. Climatic change has also to be factored in.

(iii) For big cities and its satellite towns, the water source-points are common. The feasibility of sharing water from a Water Grid on a cost sharing basis may be explored.

(iv) Information network on the quality of water and infrastructure facilities on water testing qualities are to be put in place.

(v) The water retention capacity of big reservoirs built in the bygone years need to be augmented where re-excavation would be more cost effective on consideration of economics of return of additional water from such investment.

Climate

Climate change is now the most defining challenge of mankind. It is a process of long term change of weather pattern. Such climatic change has already set in and beginning to transform life pattern on earth. Seasons are shifting, temperatures are climbing and sea levels are rising. Some of the damage consequences of climate change, which impact on our life and our surroundings may be short listed as below:

- High temperature
- Changing landscape
- Increasing risks of drought, fire and flood
- Stronger storms and increased storm-damage
- Rising seas
- Wildlife and biodiversity loss
- More heat related illness and diseases
- Economic loss

In the context of our rural economy, the impact of climate change on agriculture is very crucial. Agriculture is highly sensitive to climate variability such as drought, floods, severe storms and other seasonal stresses. Climatic change impacts agriculture instantly including its effects on crops, livestock, weeds, pests, pathogens, etc. Despite technological advances such as improved variety of seeds and irrigation system, weather does play a significant factor on availability of water -both surface and ground water and affects other crucial soil properties. As a matter of fact, the effect of climatic change on agriculture is related to variabilities in local climate rather than global climatic pattern. Consequently, assessment of climatic change on each local area is very important. The effect of climatic change on agriculture may take place in several ways as below:

(i) productivity in terms of quantity and quality of crops.

(ii) agricultural practices, through changes of water use and agricultural inputs such as herbicide, insecticide and fertilizers.

(iii) environmental effects, in particular in relation to frequency and intensity of soil drainage, soil erosion and crop diversity.

The upshot of the above discussion is that climate change has assumed critical planning issues in the area of mitigation and adaptation and decentralised local bodies need to address them based on local level variability status of climate change. As mentioned earlier, the Article 243ZD has empowered the DPC to ensure that the level of Panchayats and Municipalities need to take environmental issues under consideration at the stage of their planning exercise. It may be worthwhile to mention that climatic change related issues are not mere Planning issues; it transcends beyond that as it impacts the living environment of the local area. Very soon it might turn out as a robust challenge for decentralised bodies in some sensitive locations and pose a key governance issue of local governments.

Gender Issues

Gender has emerged as an important planning issue at all levels of planning including the decentralised level connected as it is with inclusiveness, empowerment and the MDG. It has linkage with the devolved responsibility of the decentralised local bodies. However, no structured Gender Plan as such has come into being either at the national level or at the state level except under the State Annual Plan where it is required to submit Women Component in Annexure IXA (financial) and IXB (physical) to the Planning Commission. Capturing such components does not automatically lend itself to a creditable Gender Plan. A fully blown State Gender Plan could have been a reference guide for a functional District Gender Plan. However, the State Plan is meant for line departments of the government and not for the Rural or Urban local bodies. In real terms, the Gender Plan for the levels of Panchayats or the Municipalities would depend upon the kind of devolution and its connectedness with gender. Accordingly, there would be different and distinct Gender Plan at such levels. In view of the limited devolution scenario across the states, it would be rather difficult to have uniform Gender Plan at any level.

Be that as it may, the following items need to be appropriately included under Gender Plan at the decentralised level:

Livelihood :

(a) Wage employment in general and dedicated schemes for the women, in particular, (b) Self employment and market linked initiatives, (c) Skill development and skill based employment, (d) Pension for the aged and the old age home.

Education :

(a) Gender gap in literacy, (b) Residential facilities for girl students in educationally backward districts, (c) Book grant, merit scholarship etc. for economically backward students, (d) Required toilet and boundary facilities, (e) Vocational education and vocational counselling centre.

Health :

(a) Pre-natal and Post-natal care including new born care, (b) Stoppage of female foeticide and implementation of Preconception & PNDT Act, (c) Adolescent health care, (d) Nutrition care on life cycle basis, (e) HIV and AIDS related issues.

Social Sector:

(a) Network of crèches, (b) prevention of child marriage and dowry, (c) Institutional care for the destitute and the women in distress, (d) Counselling care networks for domestic violence, trafficking, migration of women harassment in work places and other regulatory issues.

Tribal Sub-Plan (TSP) and Schedule Caste Sub-Plan (SCSP)

The welfare of the Schedule Castes and the Schedule Tribes has been an important area on planning and the Planning

Commission has been addressing this issue for long under the State Plan. The Tribal Sub-Plan (TSP) as a planning strategy has been taken up since 1974 to ensure adequate flow of plan resources for the development of Scheduled Tribes while the Special Component Plan for Scheduled Castes (SCP) has been in force since 1979-80 to ensure proportionate flow of plan resources for the development of Scheduled Castes. The SCP has been renamed as Scheduled Caste Sub Plan (SCSP) since 2006.

The broad criteria for categorisation of any schemes as SCSP or TSP are as follows:

(a) Only those schemes should be included under SCSP or TSP which ensure **direct benefits** to individuals or families belonging to Scheduled Castes or Scheduled Tribes

(b) Outlay for Area oriented schemes directly benefiting Scheduled castes hamlets/villages having more than 40% Scheduled Castes or Scheduled Tribes population shall be included in SCSP or TSP, as the case may be.

The existing guidelines further require to :

(a) earmark funds under SCSP/TSP from the State Plan outlay, at least in proportion of percentage of SC and ST population as per census, 2001.

(b) Place funds earmarked for SCSP under a separate Minor Head '789' and for TSP under Minor Head '796' below the functional major Head/Sub-Major Heads to ensure their non-divertibility to any other scheme.

The scope for separate SCSP and TSP for decentralised plans, in line to those under State Plan, has been under debate for quite some time. This is connected with hard facts of regional diversity and relative human development deficit. Further, it is also linked with constitutional mandate. The Eleventh Schedule of the Constitution of India is meant for functional items of the Panchayat but its actual position depends when the concerned State legislature formally devolves them in favour of the respective tier of Panchayats. Under item no 27 of the Eleventh Schedule of the Constitution of India, there is provision for 'Welfare of the weaker sections, in particular, of the Schedule Castes and the Schedule Tribes. In the Twelfth Schedule meant for the Municipalities, in item no 9, there is provision for 'safeguarding the interests of weaker sections of society, including the handicapped and mentally retarded. Incidentally, social welfare, including welfare of the handicapped and mentally retarded is a separate item no 26 under the Eleventh Schedule. In other words, there is specific mandate for the welfare of Schedule Castes and the Schedule Tribes for the levels of Panchayats. There is no such specific constitutional direction for the Municipalities for such categories except under general term weaker section.

Given the constitutional provision accompanied with regional diversity of varying SC and ST population and also devolution, it may not be practicable to have uniform SCSP and TSP across the tiers of the Panchayats or of the Municipalities through out the country. Additionally, conceptual difference between Plan and Sub-Plan is also important. In a system of Sub-plan, there is a stipulation to earmark a certain percentage of Plan Outlay for schemes under the Sub-Plan. Incidentally, only the Planning Commission has the prerogative to decide about Sub-Plan and that it is not in a position to interfere for sub-plan decision for the decentralised local bodies. However, beneficiaries oriented schemes for SC and ST or area oriented cluster schemes need to be taken up wherever it is possible with utmost sincerity. Additionally, human development deficit for these social groups need also to be kept in mind while planning for them. In other words, though it may not be possible to have local body specific SCSP or TSP in general, the spirit behind the same need to be addressed by incorporating dedicated schemes to ensure inclusive development for SC or ST.

Monitoring Issues Related to Planning at the Decentralised Level

The planning Commission very often sets targets for the states of India to ensure that the implementation process of the

Table 3.1: State-specific Monitorable targets for the Eleventh Five Year Plan

Tables	*Bihar*	*Madhya Pradesh*	*Uttar Pradesh*	*Rajasthan*	*Chattis-garh*	*Jharkhand*	*Orissa*
(i) Adjusted Additional Jobs (ii) Jobs needed (iii) Difference	(i) 4936764 (ii) 5777606 (iii) 840842	(i) 5167944 (ii) 4405955 (iii) -761989	(i) 12312892 (ii) 111554438 (iii) -1157454	(i) 3984290 (ii) 4695431 (iii) 711142	(i) 2089766 (ii) 1490527 (iii) 599240	(i) 2126120 (ii) 2228551 (iii) 102431	(i) 2056073 (ii) 3457021 (iii) 1400948
IMR	61 to 29	79 to 38	72 to 35	67 to 32	60 to 29	49 to 24	77 to 37
MMR	371 to 123	279 to 126	517 to 172	670 to 148	379 to126	371 to 123	358 to 119
TFR	4.3 to 2.2	3.8 to 2.4	4.4 to 2.8	3.9 to 2.2	3.8 to 2.4	4.3 to 2.2	2.6 to 1.9
Malnutrition	54.4 to 27.2	5 5.1 to 27.6	51.7 to 25.9	50.6 to 25.3	5 5.1 to 27.6	54.4 to 27.2	54-4 to 27.2
Anaemia	63.4 to 31.7	54.3 to to 27.2	48.7 to 24.4	48.5 to 24.3	54.3 to to 27.2	63.4 to 31.7	63.0 to 31.5
Sex Ratio	942 to 950	932 to 940	916 to 924	909 to 917	975 to 983	965 to 973	953 to 961
School Drop-out	78.03 to 27.85	46.81 to 16.08	42.84 to 17.96	68.50 to 29.47	46.81 to 9.95	78.03 to 29.70	61.72 to 31.9[illegible]
Literacy Rate	46.96 to 64.o4	63.72 to 84.50	56.23 to 77.20	60.43 to 79.57	64.69 to 86.16	53.52 to 70.56	63.10 to 83.9[illegible]
Gender Gap	26.6 to 17.4	25.8 to 16.3	26.6 to 13.4	31.9 to 25.6	25.5 to 15.6	28.4 to 23.0	24.8 to 15.1

Sources : N-11016/4(6)/ 2005-PC, Planning Commisssion.

five year plan is on right track. The targets are set for the state as a whole. It is meant for the line departments of the government and other partners in the state. Accordingly, it is for the state to disaggregate them among its line departments, DPCs and other programme partners. For the targets set for any DPC, it is required to further disaggregate them panchayat and Municipality wise. It is a fact that such a target setting from top is against the very spirit of decentralisation and the basis of these target setting is not always above inconvertible logic. However, reaching the targets with combined efforts of all programme partners would stand in good stead to reach the avowed goals of five year plan of the country. Based on this spirit of accommodation, it is worthwhile to address these targets on the basis of realities of life as available in the Panchayat and Municipalities in the district and set provisional targets for them to achieve the same. The DPC can take this role and set the target as objectively as possible.

The Planning Commission sets monitoring targets with the launching of a new five year plan. It is in this spirit that monitorable targets were fixed for the Eleventh Five Year Plan also for the states of India. By an example, state specific target for seven states is shown in Table 3.1.

The moot point in relation to these targets is that it has to be disaggregated district wise and then further broken down for the Panchayats and the Municipalities to enable appropriate address by such programme partners in course of planning.

Monitorable Items at Decentralized Level-Twenty Point Programme-2006

The Twenty point programme-1986 has been restructured in 2006 in conformity with the priorities of the Government. It consists of 20 points and 66 monitorable items. Out of 66 items, 25 items are monitored on monthly basis and the remaining on annual basis. It aims to the benefit of the rural and urban people. The Twenty Points and number of monitorable items under each category are indicated as follows :

1. Poverty Eradication (6 items), 2. Power to the People (3 items), 3. Support to Farmers (5 items), 4. Labour Welfare (4 items), 5. Food Security (1 item-3 components), 6. Housing for All (2 items), 7. Clean Drinking Water (2 items) 8. Health for All (8 items) 9. Education for All (2 items) 10. Welfare of Schedule Castes, Schedule Tribes, Minorities and OBCs (10 items) 11. Women Welfare (2 items) 12. Child Welfare (2 items). 13. Youth Development (3 items), 14. Improvement of Slums (1 item) 15. Environment Protection and Afforestation (3 items) 16. Social Security (2 items) 17. Rural Roads (1 item) 18. Energization of Rural Area (6 items) 19. Development of Backward Areas (1 item) 20.IT enabled e-Governance (2 items)

For the purpose of ranking the performance of States under TPP-2066 on monthly basis, the following 15 items are taken into consideration:

1, Food Security:
   (i) Targeted Public Distribution System
   (ii) Antodaya Anna Yojana
2. Rural Housing –Indira Awaas Yojana
3. EWS/LIG Houses in Urban Areas
4. Rural Areas
   - Accelerated Rural Water Supply Programme
5. Immunisation of Children
6. Sanitation Programme in Rural Areas
7. SC Families Assisted
8. ST Families Assisted
9. Universalisation of ICDS Scheme
10. Functional Anganwadis
11. Afforestation
   (i) Area Covered under Plantation-Public and Forest Lands
   (ii) Number of Seedlings planted on- Public and Forest Lands
12. Rural Roads-PMGSY
13. Rajiv Gandhi Grameen Vidyutikaran Yojana
14. Energising Pump sets

15. Supply of Electricity

While all monitorable items are important for ensuring outcome of plan initiatives, the fifteen monitorable items, as mentioned above, are crucial from assessing overall performances of the state. The decentralized local bodies also administer some of these items as part of their devolved responsibilities. It is important that performances on these important areas should also be monitored by them and share the same with the DPC and the State Government.

The upshot of the discussion is that each of the tiers of the Panchayats and the Municipalities need to give due emphasis on them at the stage of planning and should also have a distinct monitoring framework for tracking its performance based on devolved and assigned responsibilities. Since devolution is state specific, it would be useful to have a monitoring format separately for Village Panchayats, Block Panchayats and Zilla Panchayat and the Municipalites for each state. The State Planning Board and the DPCs may take lead role in designing a comprehensive monitoring check list separately for each tier of the Panchayats and Municipalities.

4

Requisites for the District Planning

Planning is a professional job and requires a lot of essential inputs including knowledge and expertise of the persons on the job. It is more so when the onus of such planning devolves on to the people's representatives. It encompasses economic and social life of the vast majority of rural and urban population living in far away places from the state head quarter. The importance is further heightened by the fact that the Indian Constitution has been amended twice (Seventy Third and Seventy Fourth Amendments) to entrust planning functions to the elected rural and urban local bodies and empowered the District Planning Committee to consolidate the same. The enormous responsibility to plan for local areas is a great challenge and also an opportunity to formulate realistic grassroots level plan for the people by their own representatives.

Incidentally, the planning functions for these grassroots areas were hitherto performed by the departments of the State Government. The transfer of such authority to units of local governments is a paradigm shift and necessitates a lot of formalities to be put in place by the Government to discharge planning functions by such local bodies. Some of such formalities have been expressly incorporated in the Constitution itself while there are others which the respective State Government need to ensure to actualise the mandate of the Constitution. It would be relevant to discuss the constitutional provisions connected with the issue at the first place.

Empowerment on Planning

The Constitution of India under Article 243G has required the State Legislature to empower the levels of Panchayats as institutions of self-governments and enacted the devolution of powers and responsibilities separately for each tier of Panchayats and empowered them with authority to prepare plans for economic development and social justice for items included in the Eleventh Schedule. Similarly, the Constitution has also provided under Article 243W that the State Legislature may enact devolution to enable the Municipalities to function as institutions of self-government and perform responsibilities for the preparation of plans for economic development and social justice for items included in the Twelfth Schedule.

The first requisite for decentralisation of planning is to be met by the concerned State Government by way of enactment of the State Panchayat Act and the State Municipal Act in terms of directives of the Constitution for clear devolution of powers and authorities on each tier of Panchayats under the Eleventh Schedule and to the Municipalities under the Twelfth Schedule to enable to plan on them.

Financial Resources for the Plan

The Constitution of India was aware of the need for resource support for plan related activities for the decentralised local bodies. There is in fact one to one correspondence and linkage between resources and functional role of an organisation and its viability. This is more so when the level of Panchayats and the Municipalities are required to implement a lot of schemes under the Eleventh Schedule and the Twelfth Schedule respectively. The Constitution enshrined defined provisions how resources are to be made available to them, some of which are indicated below:

(i) Award of the State Finance Commission Grant

The Constitution has provided that the State government shall constitute a Finance Commission under Article 243I and 243Y at the expiration of every fifth year to review the financial positions of the Panchayats and Municipalities and make recommendations, among other things, the distribution of net proceeds of the taxes, duties, tolls and fees leviable by the State. Such proceeds are to be significant financial resources for the planning of the concerned tiers of the Panchayats and the Municipalities for their respective devolved items.

The SFC is also required to recommend on taxes, fees, etc which the levels of Panchayats and the Municipalities can impose to generate resources of their own for implementation of schemes.

(ii) Award of the Central Finance Commission Grant under Article 280

The Constitution has also provided that the Central Finance Commission while giving its recommendations for the Union and the State governments on sharing of collection of proceeds from Central taxes, duties, etc. under Article 280, may also recommend for augmentation of Consolidated Fund of a state to supplement resources for the Panchayats and the Municipalities. Such awards have been made both in the Twelfth Finance Commission and also in the Thirteenth Finance Commission and constitute a corpus of fund available for the Panchayats and the Municipalities for implementation of schemes.

Devolution and Clarity on Devolution

Based on the constitutional authority on issues connected with the List-II of the Seventh Schedule of the Constitution of

India, the concerned State Government has to decide on the architecture of planning in the State including those of the decentralised planning units as per the enabling provisions of Articles 243G and 243W of the Constitution. As a matter of fact, the items covered in the Eleventh and the Twelfth Schedule of Constitution are also very much parts of the items covered in List-II and also List-III of the Seventh Schedule-the exclusive functional items for the State Government. For devolution of functional authorities, the state government has to decide what part of functional items should be divested out of his own. Further, while deciding for consideration of devolution for the Panchyat under the Eleventh Schedule and for the Municipality under the Twelfth Schedule on devolution for units of local governments, generic nature of functional items of the Eleventh and the Twelve Schedule needs to be spelt out clearly and unambiguously in functional language. The clarity on functional items and its pragmatic disaggregation determines the quality of devolution. It also shapes the functional and institutional image of the local bodies.

The meaning of devolution is thus very important in this scenario. The Constitution of India has not defined devolution as such. The absence of any clear definition on devolution has given rise to plural understandings on devolution among stake holders leading to a state of confusion across the States. Devolution is very often equated with agency function and assignment of schemes. Such understanding has not helped in the growth of local governments. The possible correct meaning of devolution, as accepted by the international community, may be found in the Human Development Report, 1993 published by the UNDP. It states that of the three forms of decentralisation namely, de-concentration, delegation and devolution, the strongest form of decentralization is devolution. It empowers decision-making powers to local authorities and allowing them to take full responsibility without reference back to government. This includes financial power as well as the authority to design and execute local development projects and programmes. The said statement points out three components of devolution namely.

(a) functional autonomy in respect of defined subjects for decision taking;
(b) financial autonomy on resource raising; and
(c) implementation autonomy on schemes designed by them;

This framework of devolution is linked with preparation of annual plan of the local bodies and is the most important requisite for meaningful District Planning. It is essential that operational modalities for devolution need to be discussed in details:

Operational Modalities

(i) Functional mapping in between the State Government and the Panchayats over items of the Eleventh Schedule and with the Municipalities over items of the Twelfth Schedule and its notification.

The Constitution of India through the Seventy third and the Seventy fourth Amendments ushered in the institutions of local governance with a future shaping mission. It is hoped that the local governments at the decentralised levels would be in a position to meet the felt needs of the local people and address the rising expectations on areas of human development. In ensuring that local governments do not exist in paper, it has been given constitutional character and enumerated provisions under different Articles of the Constitution to ensure that Local Governments are not interfered and disturbed by the mighty State Government's departments.

In furtherance to the said objective, the Constitution of India defined Panchayats and Municipalities in the first place under Article 243 and Article 243P respectively and declared them as institutions of self-government. The powers, authority and responsibilities of the Panchayats and the Municipalities have then been enumerated under Article 243G and Article 243W separately for them.

Under Article 243G, the State Government needs to empower Panchayats, at the appropriate level (i.e Village Panchayats, Block Panchayats and Zilla Panchayat) with devolution of powers and responsibilities. That is to say, Village Panchayats, Block Panchayats and Zilla Panchayat would have to be empowered with distinct and defined functions and responsibilities. For that matter, such tier of Panchayats would not require to depend on the mercy of interpretation either of any functionary in the Government or of any level of Panchayat. There is not to exist also any subordinate relationship among the tiers of Panchayats since no local self- government can be subordinate to any other local self- government.

In identical manner, the State Government is also required to empower the Municipalities under Article 243W of the Constitution with devolution of powers and responsibilities to function as institutions of local self-government.

The devolution of powers and responsibilities is future shaping as it would ultimately determine the functioning character of the local self- governments. This is indeed a very difficult area connected with federal responsibility of the state, democratic mandate obtained by the State Government on governance issues and the Constitutional obligations to perform duties on items of the Seventh Schedule (List II- State List and also List III- Concurrent List). The Constitution makers were aware of the delicate nature of function sharing and, therefore, decided that the nature of devolution in favour of such Local Governments would be decided by the concerned State Legislature based upon the objective reality and compulsion in the State. As already mentioned, the Eleventh Schedule or the Twelfth Schedule derives its functional power from the Seventh schedule itself.

Having regard to the delicate nature of devolution and also having regard to plural possibilities of devolution across the states of India on diversity considerations, the Constitution of India has enumerated a list of items (twenty nine) for the Panchayats under Eleventh Schedule and a separate list of items (eighteen) for the Municipalities under Twelfth Schedule to minimise conflict of interests in its functioning areas. There might be variation of devolution from one state to another but that the items need to belong to those covered under the Eleventh or the Twelfth Schedule, as the case may be.

The devolution of powers and responsibilities need also to be looked from other administrative and procedural angles. The State Government publishes notification of Rules of Business for the departments of the State Government under Article 166(3) of the Constitution indicating therein the kind of business that would be performed by the respective line departments in the State as per the List II-State List of the Seventh Schedule. This is the most crucial area for effecting devolution. Unless the items meant for either of the Panchayats or the municipalities are excluded from the purview of Rules of Business of the line departments, the devolution would not have any functional meaning. Otherwise, the department of the State Government would have concurrent jurisdiction over the same items with the Panchayats or the Municipalities which is just the opposite of the concept of devolution as enshrined under Article 243G or 243W of the Constitution of India. Herein lies the importance of the concept of functional mapping.

The functional mapping in this context means that subject areas of any items e.g. drinking water would have different layers of functional components meant for the Nodal department of the State Government, different tiers of the Panchayats and also for the Municipalities. Unless the functional components of programme partners on drinking water are mapped out, it would not be possible to work out confusion-free realistic devolution in between the line departments of the Government and the units of local governments in the Panchayats or the Municipalities. Further, there are common items in the Eleventh and the Twelfth Schedule on Education, Health and Sanitation, Drinking water, Roads, Energy, Poverty Alleviation and Welfare of the Weaker Sections. All these items, as mentioned earlier, are also administered by the departments of the State Government under its Constitutional obligations. All Constitutional partners-the line departments of the State Government, the Panchayats and the Municipalities-need to have clearly demarcated functional items, as per their relevant Schedule, which will be the basis for its planning, implementation and monitoring. Devolution is the only way to effect defined and distinct powers and responsibilities among the departments in the Government, the Panchayats and the Municipalities. Detailing of such components and its function-wise role mapping would be a *sine qua non* for pragmatic devolution.

Another area related to functional mapping is those covered under Centrally Sponsored Schemes or the Central Sector Schemes being implemented at the rural or urban areas in a state. The Centrally Sponsored Schemes fall in the jurisdiction of Concurrent list and are funded by the Central Government and the State Government on a shared basis (i.e. 90%-10%, 80%-20%, 75%-25%, 50%-50% etc.) There could be 100% contribution of such scheme by the Central Government as well e.g. National Family Planning Programme. The Central sector schemes are funded and implemented by the agencies of the Central Government. In some cases, it is also implemented by the agencies of the State Government including the tiers of Panchayats or the Municipalities e.g. NAREGA, MPLAD, etc., Incidentally, it may be mentioned that the Central Government is not empowered to assign such schemes either to any tier of the Panchayat or to the Municipalities as the subjects of Panchayat and the Municipality fall under the State List. Assignment of any scheme to the Panchayats or the Municipalities by the Central Government has to take the route of prior concurrence of the concerned State Government.

The upshot of the discussion is that depending on devolution vision of the State, the State Government needs to curve out exclusive jurisdiction of works for the Panchayats and the Municipalities and exclude the said works from the Rules of Business for its own departments published under

Article 166(3) of the Constitution. This will settle once for all the issue of jurisdiction on areas of planning and implementation for the Governments and the local self-governments. The respective planning authority would then have clear ideas of exclusive jurisdiction of work areas for which they would plan and implement independently. The clarity on planning is an essential perquisite for confusion-free local level planning and would help its consolidation by the District Planning Committee.

(ii) Functional mapping on devolved items under the Eleventh Schedule among the Gram Panchayat, Block Panchayat and Zilla Panchayat and its notification.

Devolution of functions and responsibilities among the three tiers of Panchayats is the most difficult area. This is also an area where the depth of confusion is alarmingly high. Article 243G requires that there has to take place clearly defined functions for the levels of Panchayats. Therefore, the functions and responsibilities of the Village Panchayat, Block Panchayat and Zilla Panchayat would have to be distinct and different from one another. The functional identity and its performance would determine the very growth of local self-governments at the levels of the Panchayats.

For effecting devolution among the tiers of Panchayats it would be necessary to have detailed functional break-up for the items so devolved to the Panchayats as a whole and then map its components as Village-centric, Block-centric or District-centric. The relevance of functional areas, its possible interconnectedness and the availability of infrastructural support etc, are to be factored in for decision on devolution. At this stage, the principle of subsidiarity as recommended by the Second Administrative Reforms Commission for devolution may be given due consideration. The Second Administrative Reforms Commission recorded its recommendations at para 2.2.3 as below:

"The principle of subsidiarity stipulate: functions shall be carried out closest to citizens at the smallest unit of governance possible and delegated upwards only when the local unit cannot perform the task."

The philosophy of subsidiarity may have its overarching consideration for decision on devolution, but other important ground realities have also to be given their appropriate weightage e.g. the load-bearing capacity of the first tier of local governance does have its own institutional limitations. Besides, other tiers of Panchayats are required to perform Constitution mandated role as institutions of local self-governments. Incidentally, empowerment of the tiers of Panchayat can not proceed by trial and error of success or failure. It would be fair and equitable if devolution is settled based on state vision, its philosophy on devolution, the ground realities of the maturity of the tiers of Panchayats as institutions, the outer limit of load bearing management capability of concerned tiers of Panchayats and other factors, as appropriate.

Another area of caution in this area is the super-hyped noise of activity mapping. Activity mapping and functional mapping are two different concepts. Functional mapping, as earlier mentioned, is a kind of listing of possible functions relevant for decision on devolution. Activity mapping on the other hand is an exercise to catalogue activities relevant to perform any task or defined function e.g. implementation of scheme. Functional mapping is an essential requisite for effective devolution while activity mapping is an exercise for quality performance of any work.

The caution to link activity mapping as a platform for devolution arises because some of the State Governments mention it as essential requisite for roadmap to devolution. Activities are causal factors while function is the sum total of effects of activities. Function is indeed the outcome of sum of activities. Disagrregation of activities among the tiers of Panchayats would imply subdivision of a whole of functional responsibilities. Thus, Activity based delineation of functions among the tiers of Panchayat strikes at the very core of local self-government and perforce subordinate functional relationship among the tiers of Panchayat –an area totally alien to the high valued concept of devolution, as enshrined in the Article 243G.

Further, activity based planning is a novel concept of part planning, a discrete form of planning exercise. The very idea of relaying the baton of performance of one activity of one tier on to the next tier is any thing but practical. The dependence on time sequenced performance of an activity of another tier brings in its turn dependence syndrome, uncertainty and tension in the area of programme implementation. Besides, when such activity is linked with a number of units of one tier (i.e.Gram Panchayats) to another tier (say, Block Panchayat), the chance of performance of complementary activity by the next tier becomes all the more uncertain in a time-line. Further, budgeting for activities of a part of a scheme across the tiers of Panchayat is an unusual concept and hardly implementable. Needless to mention, output of a scheme is a wholesome concept and depends on performance of all activities. It would be wise to guard against romantic illusion of activity mapping and fall in the trap of quick- sands of confusion.

The nature of devolution for local governments in our country is still at its nascent and transitional stage and would require some more time to firm-up. Meanwhile, the tiers of Panchayats are mostly vested with assigned responsibility, either formally or in an informal arrangement, for execution of schemes. Such schemes may belong to Flagship programmes of the Central Government i.e. NAREGA or it may as well belong to State Government programmes i.e. distribution of minikits for different crops to the local farmers. In order to ensure focussed role in planning and implementation by local self-governments, it is absolutely necessary that the tiers of Panchayats are empowered with clear, distinct and independent functioning roles where the nature of function would itself serve as a brand image for the particular tier of Panchayats.

The upshot of the discussion is that the units of local level planning would have to know for certain what is to be planned. Such items for planning need to come from the Eleventh Schedule under devolved Constitutional responsibilities as per Constitutional mandate. The State is to ensure that the units of Panchayats would know for certain the specified subjects meant for their governance. Such clarity and clear delineation of functions would help them to plan in a focussed way and implement in a proper manner to achieve intended output. Devolution does not allow concurrent responsibility of the same job by all the tiers of Panchayat at the same time.

(D) Conceptual Clarifications on District Planning Committee vis-a-vis parastatal agencies -the statutory Development Authorities and the Non-statutory Development Board.

The mighty challenge of development deficit, bridging the rural urban divide, land use based planning, inclusive growth for the marginalised and the urge to develop satellite township etc, led to the growth of different forms of institutions including parastatal agencies, both statutory and non-statutory, in different states. Some of them existed even prior to the Seventy Third and Seventy Fourth Amendments of the Constitution and continued till date. Some of such organisations came into existence after the Seventy Third and Seventy Fourth Amendments on grounds of compulsions of the state governance. The programmes and planning of these parastatal agencies, which work in isolation in a defined zone, do have impact on the institutions of local self-governments and the District Planning Committee. These institutions have created problems of duality in planning area, both subject-wise and area-wise. It has also spawned in the process stand-alone pockets of development, unconnected with the Constitution mandated local self-governments. The issue of mainstreaming such parastatal agencies with appropriate unit of the local self-government needs to be addressed as a part of sectoral reforms in the local government areas.

The existence of parastatal agencies could have been justified if the State Governments entrusted them with non-devolved subjects covered under State List and being implemented by the departments of the State Government. In that event it would have nothing to infringe with subjects covered under the Eleventh Schedule or the Twelfth Schedule of the Constitution. The parastatal agencies perform almost identical functional subjects as are admissible to the Panchayats or the Municipalities. The duality in the role of planning and implementation is neither good for the local self-governments nor is it honourable for the parastatal agencies to encroach upon the Constitution mandated area of the Panchayats or the Municipalities.

Given the hard fact that the growth of the Panchayats and the Municipalities has not been uniformly fair, such parastatal agencies might exist as a part of planning reality for the time being .Pending reforms in this area by the concerned State, it is necessary to take them along for some time more and minimize the areas of conflict as far as possible. Since such parastatal agencies function at the district level, it would make sense that they may be asked by the State Government to share their areas of work, its geographical location and details of plan etc, in each year with the District Planning Committee at the planning stage for avoidance of duplication of efforts, for institutionalising transparency in its functioning areas and also for effecting rewarding relationship, where ever possible. The District Planning Committee may, in turn, share the information, so provided, with the concerned tiers of the Panchayat or the Municipalities for appropriate guidance. It would also be desirable to capture planning profiles of such parastatal agencies in a separate section under the District Plan and its outcome profiles in the Annual Report of the District Planning Committee.

(E) Clarity on Planning Jurisdiction between the District Planning Committee and the Metropolitan Planning Committee.

The planning jurisdiction between the Metropolitan Planning Committee and the District Planning Committee has been posing conceptual queries every now and then. It centred on dual authority of the District Planning Committee and the Metropolitan Planning Committee over a part of the defined geographical jurisdiction. The District Planning Committee is required to consolidate plans prepared by the Panchayats and the Municipalities and prepare the Draft Development Plan. In exercise of that power it enjoys supervisory authority in relation to plans prepared by units of such local self-governments. In furtherance of that role, it may guide such units of Panchayats and Municipalities in respect of envisioning process, stock taking of natural and other resources, taking a look on development deficit including human development deficit, convergence related issue connected with planning and finally on leveraging national priorities, state priorities, district priorities and local government priorities as reflected in the felt needs of people. The scope for outside interference by the Metropolitan Planning Committee does not exist.

The Constitution of India enshrined the Metropolitan Planning Committee under Article 243ZE with due regard to the existence of District Planning Committee for consolidation of plans prepared by the Panchayats and the Municipalities .The Metropolitan Planning Committee (MPC) has been designed to play a different professional and coordinating role on planning in the context of fast racing development initiatives in the Metropolitan cities of the country. The Article 243ZE (3) provides:

Every Metropolitan Planning Committee shall, in preparing the draft development plan,-

(a) have regard to-
   - (i) the plans prepared by the Municipalities and the Panchayats in the Metropolitan area;
   - (ii) matters of common interest between the Municipalities and the Panchayats, including coordinated spatial planning of the area, sharing of water and other physical and natural resources, the integrated development of infrastructure and environmental conservation;

(iii) the overall objectives and priorities set by the Government of India and the Government of the State;

(iv) the extent and nature of investments likely to be made in the Metropolitan area by agencies of the Government of India and the Government of the State and other available resources whether financial or otherwise;

(b) Consult such institutions and organisations as the Governor may, by order, specify.

It would appear that the Constitution of India has not mentioned any word like District Plan or the District Planning Committee on anything connected with Metropolitan Planning. It has instead enshrined that the Metropolitan Planning Committee (MPC) may take into consideration of plans prepared by such of Panchayats and Municipalities, who fall in the metropolitan region, for possible reference in the preparation of draft development plan. There is nothing in the Constitution for the MPC to encroach upon the authority of the DPC or to interfere with the planning exercises of either the Panchayats or the Municipalities at any stage of planning. For preparation of an objective plan at the level of MPC, it has been empowered to take a holistic view on matters of common interest- with Panchayats and Municipalities - including spatial planning and sharing of water and other natural resources, on integrated development of infrastructure and environmental conservation. Therefore, the myth of duality of planning control over the Panchayats and the Municipalities by the District Planning Committee and the Metropolitan Planning Committee is not real. In matters relating to planning, the Panchayats and the Municipalities are guided by the District Planning Committee only as provided under Article 243ZD.

There is one very significant point, implicit in the Constitutional provision, that distinguishes plans prepared by the Panchayats and the Municipalities from that of the Metropolitan Planning Committee. The Metropolitan Planning cannot just commence it real works unless the draft Panchayat plans and the draft Municipal plans of the relevant areas are prepared and made ready. Otherwise, the Metropolitan Plan would miss out a forum for its reality check. From that angle, the timelines of metropolitan planning has obviously to be different from the timelines of planning of the Panchayats or of the Municipalities.

Further, the Planning Commission requires that the Annual state plan should be accompanied by Annual District Plans. Such Annual District Plans are supposed to serve as sub-sets of the Annual State Plan. No such stipulation is, however, made in respect of the Metropolitan Plan. A Metropolitan Plan appears to be truly in the category of perspective plan and has to be prepared by interaction with larger audiences-the Central government, the State government, other financial institutions and organisations, apart from the Panchayats and the Municipalities.

(F) Sequencing timelines of planning for all the tiers of the Panchayats, Municipalities and District Planning Committee in relation to the timelines of the State Plan as fixed by the Planning Commission

One of the crucial items for Planning is its time components. There are broadly two aspects related to time for planning:

(i) Time required for proper planning;

(ii) Time-line within which the plan is required to be submitted.

The planning machinery everywhere usually remains tuned on overarching issues of planning throughout the year. The usual expectation is that such machinery, even though limited and variously qualified at any level of DPC and of the local bodies, need to be at their concurrent mode on tracking planning issues throughout year. The resultant knowledge and updated data would stand in good stead in addressing planning issues comprehensively and in time. The real world field situation is never perfect and it explains why the planning exercises do not take off at the right time inviting time pressure for completion of a serious job in time. For that single reason, the quality of planning is often compromised. It promotes to compromise time factor by making minor changes of their previous plan. The planning area suffers from these maladies which require careful and deft handling.

Planning has a link with thinking process of knowledge workers and stakeholders. It is concerned with today as much as it concerns for tomorrow. The problems of current real life need comprehensive resolution but space for future development should also be kept in mind at the same time. Plural perceptions and diversity of knowledge take their own time for social acceptance and ownership. That crucial time has to be accounted for in the time budget of planning for local bodies.

The time frame of planning exercises also depends on the load factor associated with planning. If the District Plan is to be prepared unconnected with State Plan, the time frame for planning District plan would be somewhat different. The District planning in such case need not follow up the time lines of the State Plan. The District Plans in that situation are to be prepared on the basis of devolved items based on award of the State Finance Commission, Central Finance Commission, own resources of the local bodies and other grants, if any. Even after going round the step by step approach, as per guidelines of the 'Planning at the Grassroots level', the District Planning in such situation would require relatively lesser amount of time. In view, however, of imperfect devolution obtaining in the system and that the Panchayats and Municipalities are vested with assigned responsibility of planning and implementation of State Sponsored Schemes, the inclusion of such items in the planning exercise would mean that both the Panchayats and the Municipalities need to receive or obtain required inputs including fund availability from the concerned line departments of the Government, which by itself is time taking, and consequently, the time-frame for planning would be somewhat longer.

Additionally, the Constitutional requirement of interactive consultations for Gram Panchayat plans at the level of Gram Sabha and Municipal plan at the level of Ward sabha would require time and such time component would also have to be factored in for assessment of time for planning. Additionally, in some states Block Panchayat Plan and Zilla Panchayat Plan are also to be drawn up after interactions with citizen's forums. Further, different time plan would be needed for Perspective Plan, Draft Development Plan or Five Year Plan. The timelines for Annual Plan is connected with Planning Commission's yearly circular for submission of Annual Plan and its connected timelines for approval and its budgeting thereafter by the State Government

The upshot of the above discussions on timelines in planning is that the current practice of commencement of planning exercise after receipt of circular on the Annual plan from the Planning Commission, both at the state level and at the decentralised levels, needs to be changed having regard to real time requirement for the related works. A system needs also to be built up in the administrative departments, and also at the level of decentralised local bodies, as to when the Quarterly/Half Yearly Plan Review is to be made, when the Annual Plan Review is to take place and when the next Annual Plan related interaction has to be arranged to make use of learning inputs from the reviews of the plan performances. Additionally, the time required for the process and formulation of plan proposals by three tier Panchayats and Municipalities including Municipal Corporations and its consolidation by the District Planning Committee has to be appropriately worked out and institutionalised.

Incidentally, the time concept of planning is also found in the Panchayat Act and Municipal Acts of the State. There is a statutory time-line for convening a meeting for approval of Annual Plan. However, such Acts do not mention time required for the process function of planning. The statutory time-frame for meeting on Annual Plan for the tiers of Panchayats and the

Municipalities is different from one local body to another and varies from one State to another. Such statutory time frames do not agree with time frame usually worked out by the Planning Commission for the Annual Plan for the State. Since the Planning Commission requires inputs on Rural Plan and Urban Plan in the presentation format of the State Plan -GNC-I and GNC-II the timelines for planning for such Rural and Urban local bodies have to be appropriately linked.

The Planning Commission has addressed time format with reference to District Plan as per recommendations of Committee on 'The Planning at the Grassroots Level' published in March 2006 by the Ministry of Panchayati Raj, Government of India (at page 30-31). The same Time Plan was adopted at 'Manual on Integrated District Planning' prepared by a Task Force and published by the Planning Commission, in the following manner:

Time Lines for District Planning

1. State-level Workshop for all Chairpersons, Vice-chairpersons and Member Convenors of all DPCs.—May
2. First meeting of District Planning Committee to discuss the Guidelines and constituting Sectoral Sub-Committees for preparation of District Vision and Perspective Plan.—June
3. Formulation of District Vision.— by July
4. Approval of District Vision by DPC and sending the same to all Local Bodies—July
5. District level Workshops— August
6. Block level Workshop— August
7. Meeting of Local Bodies to discuss guidelines and constituting Working Groups.——September
8. Formulation of Local Bodies' vision. ——September
9. Approval in the General Body meeting of Local Bodies.—October
10. Conducting Gram Sabha/Ward Sabha —October-November
11. Development Seminars.—— November- December

12. Preparations of Final Local Bodies' Five Year Plans by Working Groups——January
13. Consolidation of Final Local Bodies' Five Year Plans.—January
14. Submission of Local Bodies' Five Year Plans to District Planning Committee.—January
15. Discussion with representatives of Local Bodies' and approval by District Planning Committee.——February
16. Approvals by District Planning Committees- March
17. Bringing out the Development perspective of the District and Local Bodies' Five Year Plans and Annual Plans—March.

The model Time- lines give fairly good descriptions for activity- centred actions for planning. It also serves as a monitoring instrument for the officials of the District Planning Committee to follow up the time sequence and ensure its timely performance. It is worth while to note that time slippage on one area may be made good by the extra initiative in the subsequent steps. The final dateline is the most important.

The above Time- lines raise a number of queries which need to be resolved comprehensively. The top down envisioning process does not fit in with centrality of the decentralisation philosophy. Besides, it has not kept any time slot for forwarding the Draft District Plan to the nodal department of the State, as mentioned at Article 243ZD(4). Further, as earlier pointed out, the time lines incorporated under the State Panchayat Act or the State Municipal Act normally do not correspond with the time lines at the 'Manual for Integrated District Planning' published by the Planning Commission. Besides, Working Group, as mentioned, is an exogenous body and cannot usurp the statutory planning function of any local body. This unhappy situation for statutory local bodies needs to be sorted out.

The time lines for other action points at the level of Panchayats or the Municipalities ,which have not featured at the 'Manual for Integrated District Planning', need to be taken care of, namely :

1. Inputs for planning from Gram Sansad/Village development Committees/other tiers of Panchayat /Ward Committee, as applicable (where ever exists) by ——
2. Interacting session to sensor felt needs of planning priorities at the level of Gram Sabhas/ Ward Sabhas by —
3. Stock taking exercises and resource mapping by ——
4. Local body's (Village Panhayat/ Block Panchayat/ Zilla Panchayat / Municipality) first meeting on consensus building on Visioning, Human development deficit, ongoing plan performances on devolved responsibilities and assigned tasks etc.) by ——
5. Formulation of Local body's draft Annual Plan by —
6. Approval of the draft Annual Plan by the Local Body by —
7. Despatch of the draft Annual Plan to the District Planning Committee by —
8. District Planning Committee's possible observations which needed to be re-looked and reconsidered by such local body by —
9. Reconsidered plan submitted by such local body to the District Planning Committee by —
10. Time for consolidation of Panchayats plan into Rural Plan and consolidation of Municipal Plans into Urban Plan and then consolidating them as draft District Plan at the level of DPC by —

There is another category of time requirement for the Panchayats and the Municipalities before the fall of a new financial year. All local self-governments have to prepare and approve their Annual Budget in such manner as prescribed in the respective State Act. All proposals, as approved in the Annual Plan, have to be sanctioned in their own Budget with commensurate fund to enable to spend on such schemes from the beginning of the new financial year. The timelines of approval of Budget, as per statutory provision in state act, have to be taken care of. This calls for adjustment of time by way of reworking the timelines as worked out in the Manual of the District Planning.

(G) Back-up Financial Resources for the Annual Plan

The Draft District Plan in many districts turns out to be an exercise of wish-list without making any effort to locate fund for the schemes. In some cases, it boils down as indent for fund requirement. Prioritisation of developmental areas and prioritisation of schemes within that area are hardly addressed making all the exercises less meaningful, non-professional and notional. Such a casual approach on planning is neither permissible, nor does it serve the avowed objectives of planning at the grassroots level.

There is in fact direct relationship between plan proposals and the identification of funds. While plan-finance related issue of State Plan is examined and finalised by the Planning Commission, it remains more or less an illusory area for the local level Plans. The Constitution makers were alive to the requirement of fund for local governance and along with devolution of functional items, it also set up the State Finance Commission to award financial grant for the discharge of functional responsibilities. Unfortunately, most of the States have not formally devolved such functional items on to such local bodies and the awards of the State Finance Commissions also turned out as mere general purpose grant. Such award is seldom linked with items of devolution. Besides, the quantum of receivable funds for the next year is not communicated at the time of planning exercises in most of the states. Kerala happens to be the lone exception.

The other option to raise internal resources by the local bodies is through imposition of taxes, fees, rates, etc. In absence of proper enactment of fiscal power among the tiers of Panchayat and the nature of its elasticity, the resource availability for plan finance is also not encouraging. For the Municipalities, however, the macro position of internal resources is somewhat better, though in many cases it is not good enough even to meet its organisational costs. Be that as it may, resource availability from internal resources has to be factored in while calculating availability of plan finance, however, small it might be.

The Central Finance Commission also awards grant to the Local Bodies for meeting development deficit on many counts. Some components of this grant in question are also area specific. However, the allocation principle of such grant is decided by the State Government. The possible fund availability on tied programmes needs to be communicated to the concerned local bodies at the stage of Annual Plan exercises. The other possible sources of plan fund is from financial institutions-for infrastructural loan or otherwise. The details of them, as could be relied upon at the stage of planning exercise, have to be taken into consideration for the purpose resources availability for the Annual Plan.

The State Government (also the Central Government) assigns different tiers of Panchayats and the Municipalities with definite schemes. In all such cases, the State Government is required to place funds for its execution. The nature of such assigned schemes and the possible tied up fund availability need to be made known to such local bodies at the stage of planning exercise. Incidentally, the culture of sharing such information with such local bodies in time has yet to take an institutional character and the demand pull forces to share such information do not always prove effective. Such information needs to be communicated in routine manner by the related departments of the State Government.

Another aspect of plan finance also deserves special mention. The accounting system and practices of the State-finances have grown up over the years under the watchful eyes of the Accountant General of the State. In that system, the Plan Fund and Non-plan Fund are clearly differentiated by respective accounting codes and funds are provisioned accordingly. There is no scope for using plan fund for non-plan purposes and vice versa. The system of such rigorous discipline has yet to take shape in local bodies' financial administration which needs adequate sensitisation and supervision. This is very important in that it ensures that plan funds are used for implementation of plan schemes only. The Planning Commission, while according approval of the State Annual Plan, encloses a statement on the scheme of financing the Annual Plan to ensure that the Annual Plan in question would not suffer for dearth of fund. This system is not in vogue in the case of local bodies' plans. It is only desirable that such a practice evolves in the case of local bodies' plans as well. This practice would introduce a self-correcting mechanism in the planning scenario of the local bodies to pose plan proposals only when there are 'identified funds'. This is a big area for institutional reform in the financial management of local governance. In order to ensure that local bodies prepare plan proposals with identified resources, a model format indicating the scheme of financing is indicated below which needs to be appended with any Local Body's Plan:

(H) The Statement of back-up Financial Resources for the Annual Plan—(Year)

of the —(name of the local body)

(a) Projected Resources for Devolved Programmes:

1. Projected Revenue available from own sources————

1. Grant available on recommendations from the State Finance Commission on devolved items————

2. Grant available on recommendations from Central Finance Commission on (mentioned) programme :

3. Other Grants receivable from the State Governments :

(b) Projected Resources for Assigned Programmes

5. Projected funds availability for:

(i) NAREGA ————

(ii) RKVY ————

(iii) BRGF ————

(iv) SSA ————

(v) Others (please specify) ————

(c) Projected Resources for any other Non- assigned programmes

(i) —— ————

(ii) —— ————

(d) Projected Resources from Financial Institutions for Programmes:

(i) —— ————

(ii) —— ————

(e) Projected Resources from Any Other Sources/ Institutions for Programmes:

(i) Gifts/Donations ————

(ii) Interest from any Endowments ————

(f) Total Projected Fund Availability for the Annual Plan : ————

(g) Total Plan Proposals for the Annual Plan

————

(H) Amendments of the Rules of Business of the State Government under Article 166(3) of the Constitution incorporating therein such functional devolution.

The conduct of business of the Government of a State is to be carried out as per provisions under Article 166 of the Constitution. It has been provided that the State Government is required to publish Rules of Business for the transaction of the business of the State and also allocation among Ministers of the said business. The business of the State and the corresponding role of the Ministers are also organically linked with devolution of powers and responsibilities on to the Panchayats and the Municipalities. The Eleventh Schedule and the Twelfth Schedule of the Constitution derives its functional items from the Mother Schedule -the Seventh Schedule, List II -State List and also List III of the Concurrent List. It is for the same reason that the Article 243G and Article 243W provided the authority to the State Legislature to decide on the extent of the devolved functional responsibilities on to the Panchayats and Municipalities having regard to the List- II of the Seventh Schedule. Since the Ministers of the Government do not have any role directly to interfere with the functioning of Local Self-Governments, the Rules of the Business of the State Government need to ensure that those Ministers or their Officers do not interfere with the business of the Local Self-

Governments. There cannot be common functional items or concurrent jurisdiction in between the State Government and the Local Self-Governments. Local Body specific devolution, even on selective basis, would enable them to grow as institution and specialise on those areas. It will also help to evolve decentralised institutional character.

One of the reasons for halting progress on decentralisation in our country is our inability to delink functional responsibility of the Local Self-Governments from the functional responsibility of the departments of the State Government. The existence of concurrent responsibilities has been standing as a roadblock to decentralisation. This could be addressed formally by excluding devolved items from the business of the departments of the State Government by notification under Rules of Business under Article 166(3) of the Constitution. Needless to mention, it will help Local Government's programme planning, implementation and ensuring outcome. Such action would also help the growth of Local Self-Governments.

(I) Notification by the State nodal departments of State Sector Schemes, District Sector Schemes and District Sector Local Body Schemes as functionally mapped out.

As a corollary to issues connected with devolution is the concept of State Sector Schemes, District Sector Schemes and District Sector Local Body Schemes. The State Sector Schemes refer to those schemes which are very critical to the growth of the State economy and located either in the State capital region or in the districts. Usually, such schemes cover more than one district. In any event, when any scheme spreads beyond the boundary of any district, it automatically qualifies as State Sector Schemes. Further, External Aided Projects by virtue of being lumpy and the related corpus of fund being tied with a complex pattern of release of such funds along with its concurrent monitoring and reporting format, it always falls under State Sector Schemes and remain indivisible. Similarly, supertechnology based projects which are knowledge dependent and cannot normally be handled by the district level functionaries also belong to the State Sector Schemes.

The District Sector Schemes refer usually to those schemes whose territorial jurisdiction is covered within the boundaries of any district. It would lose its character as soon as the scheme in question extends beyond the district boundary. Such District Sector Schemes can broadly be divided under two categories:

(i) Local Bodies' Schemes

(ii) Line Departments' Schemes

The Local Bodies' Schemes include those schemes taken up by any of the tiers of the Panchayat, the Municipalities or the Municipal Corporations and being implemented by them while the Line Departments' Schemes indicate schemes which are being implemented by the departments of the state government in the district. Such schemes may be located in any Panchayat or Municipal area or cover both.

There is close connection of the above classification of schemes with devolution in that it brings in clarity and simplifies the areas for decision on devolution by the State Government. It will require the State to concentrate on District Sector Local Bodies' schemes only for the purpose of devolution of functions. Such a classification will also restrict the Line departments of the State not to cross over the planning boundary of the decentralised Local Bodies.

(J) Separate head of accounts for all devolved items for the Panchayats and the Municipalities and release of fund from there on.

It has earlier been mentioned that the plan schemes can be taken up for implementation when those are budgeted for. The schemes are budgeted under respective budget heads as provided by the Accountant General of the State. Normally such heads are meant for the departments of the State Government. These departments are responsible for the release of fund, book those in appropriate ledger, spend it accordingly and then place the records to the Audit team of the Accountant General of the State for verification of accounts.

In cases where devolution of functions have taken place, the concerned departments of the State Government will no longer be in a position to implement such components of devolved functions. The budgeting for such component of functions in the departmental budget is also not permissible which would other-wise mean that the department has budgeted on devolved functions which it is no longer authorised. The release of fund from departmental budget head to local governments for devolved function would also mean that the said unit of local self-government, *ipso facto*, is required to act as an implementing agency of the related department. Like any implementing agency, the unit of a local self-government is also bound to carry out all instructions of the said department on implementation, monitoring and maintenance of records and is also answerable to the department for audit of expenditure. When such a unit of local government is required to function as implementation agency of a number of departments, the myth of decentralisation and local self-governance is completely shattered.

In this given background there is a compelling reason to open up new heads of accounts for devolved items in favour of all the tiers of the Panchayats and the Municipalities in consultation with the Accountant General of the State. In fact, based on the nature of recommendations of the State Finance Commission, the State Government is required to open required number of new heads of accounts. In any case, head wise provisioning of funds would mean certainty of fund availability for devolved items for the Panchayats under the Eleventh Schedule or for the Municipalities under the Twelfth Schedule. This would strengthen the decentralisation status of the local self-governments in the State by way of assured funding support for implementation of devolved schemes.

(k) Determination of Cabinet Minister's responsibility on devolved items at the floor of the Assembly and also at the Public Accounts Committee.

The hall mark of Parliamentary System of Government is collective responsibility of the Cabinet. However, the individual Ministers are also responsible for items entrusted to them for its policy formulation, its implementation and also all items incidental thereto including its responsibility at the floor of the Assembly and also at the Public Accounts Committee. The Ministers are responsible for details of areas as are included under the Rules of Business published under Article 166(3) of the Constitution.

In situations where the State Government has effected devolution in favour of the Panchayats and the Municipalities for defined functions, as are listed in the Eleventh and Twelfth Schedule, the related Ministers will no longer be responsible in the administration of such components of functions so divested away from the department and devolved on to local self-governments. The question of vesting responsibility to any Minister for business connected with devolved functions on to local self-governments at the floor of the Assembly and also at the Public Accounts Committee is very relevant and needs comprehensive resolution. This point has not opened up into the surface so far as very few states have effected devolution formally. However, policy decision on this crucial area is also called for.

5

Rural Planning by the Tiers of Panchayats-Gram Panchayat, Block Panchayat and Zilla Panchayat

The Ministry of Panchayat, Government of India in consultation with the Planning Commission published a document 'Planning at the Grassroots level' for rural planning, in which the modalities for rural planning have been worked out. This model guidelines, which may be called the grammar of rural planning, need to be followed both in substance and in spirit in planning by the tiers of Panchayats at their local area with such minor adjustments as permissible.

The 'Planning at the Grassroots Level' suggested the following steps for the planning at the district level:

(a) **Stage-I : Building a District Vision**

Building a district vision is the first requirement of a Five Year Plan at the decentralised level. District vision is not to be developed and imposed by district level functionaries but that it needs to be formed through an interactive process by the participation of all stakeholders- the local bodies and civil societies at large- for its acceptance and ownership.

Normally such a vision would stay for a period of time, say 5- years, and that it may not lapse into a case of annual exercise. However, there is no bar if the said stakeholders meet on an annual basis to take stock of changing environment and update it accordingly.

The core vision is not to be conditioned by schemes and programmes at hand but would be primarily articulated in terms of goals and outcomes of three areas of development namely, human development, infrastructure development and development in the productive sector. The vision on human development needs to cover health, education, women and child welfare, social justice and availability of basic minimum services. The vision for infrastructure may be formed on the basis of the components of Bharat Nirman while the vision for the productive sector needs to take into consideration the potentialities in the district and what can be reached within the vision period taking into consideration the natural and human resources available in the district.

(b) Undertaking a Parallel Stock Taking Exercise

Paralleling the envisioning process, a stocktaking exercise is also to be taken up on assessment of human condition and the availability of natural, social and financial resources and infrastructure. The data so obtained could be put in a development radar, as used by the Planning Commission on preparation for the National Human Development Report, 2001, to give a pictorial description of the performance of a unit of planning in respect of health, education, poverty alleviation, drinking water, housing etc.

Such stock taking exercises need also to include physical and financial achievement of services provided by the Government and the Private Sector. Natural resources data base management as installed in the GIS system in the district need to be made use of for the related planning units of the Panchayats. In view of the importance of the Natural Resources

Data Base Management System (NRDMS) in the planning process, a paragraph is separately added.

Natural Resources Data Base Management System (NRDMS)

NRDMS has been in functional mode in almost all the district headquarters of the country. It is based on the principle of Geographic Information System (GIS) and aims at setting up district level resource database, demonstrating their ability in local level planning, developing Spatial Decision Support System (SDSS), promoting R&D in spatial data base technology and training of potential end-users.

In a scenario of large diversity of data sets, this platform assists in the use of spatial decision support tools for planning and management of resources at the local level.

The tiers of Panchayats are required to obtain relevant data for planning use from the NRDMS. Some illustrative examples are given. In the field of irrigation, the query to the NRDMS could be number, location and coverage of Ponds, Dug wells, Mini-Dug wells, Auto flow, RLI, Shallow tube wells, Deep tube wells, Field Channel etc. Regarding soil, the query could relate to types of soil, problems of soil, potential use of the soil and the like. In relation to crops, it could be area under production for paddy, wheat, pulses, vegetables, season specific production and its linkage with marginal farmers, small farmers and others. The query relating to ARD may relate to number of deshi (local) cows, hybrid cows, per capita milk production from each of the categories, its marketing outlets etc. Primary Schools relating data query may relate to number of schools, its distance from one to another, schools with one room/two rooms; for boys or girls or for both; exclusive for SC or ST; with or without drinking water facility, with or without toilets; with or without toilets for girl students, with or without play ground etc. As to the drinking water, it could be hamlets with no water source, with one or more water sources and the distance usually covered to fetch water. Queries could be varied and may range from air, sunshine, rainfall, forests, minerals, fisheries- the potential resources and its actual use.

The NRDMS data are validated with due process, updated regularly and are extremely valuable and important inputs for planning and decision on location of schemes. It gives objective and professional guidance in a situation when there are competitive claims on any planning related issues.

Knowing the Citizens

'Planning for whom' is an important issue that needs to be seriously addressed at the beginning of any planning exercise. With it is connected the inclusive development agenda of any unit of Panchayat. The census figure gives a broad overview of the structure of population which, however, needs to be further segregated in terms of children, adolescents, women and the aged. The number of physically and mentally challenged persons and the persons belonging to Schedule Castes, Schedule Tribes and other Backward Castes have also to be collected along with the number of cultivators, share croppers, agricultural workers and non-workers. The status of BPL population and the unemployed youths would also be needed for formulation of Annual Plan.

Incidentally, increasing number of population is posing the greatest threat on our planning and development. Ultimately, it is the size of population for whom programmes have to be taken up under Plan, and its increasing huge size is a positive deterrent on plan resources and on its management. All the local bodies have national duty to ensure that spurt of such additional growth has to be contained as much as possible. The local bodies need to capture population since 1951 to 2011 and keep it in the upfront to understand the magnitude of all issues connected with population. For planning purposes, even though the decadal growth is important, it is ultimately the size of the population that is to be factored in for programme intervention for economic and social development. The seriousness of the importance of size can be seen from the census figures of Murshidabad district in West Bengal, which is incidentally now a minority concentrated (63.95%) border district:

Population in Murshidabad District,West Bengal

1951	*1961*	*1971*	*1981*	*1991*	*2001*	*2011(p)*
1715759 (4.61%)	2290010 (33.46%)	2946563 (28.57%)	3697552 (25.49%)	4740149 (28.20%)	5866569 (23.76%)	7102430 (21.07%)

P- Provisional. Percentage: Decadal growth.

Source: Census of India

(i) Planning approach for the Panchayats:

The planning for any tier of the Panchayat may be looked from three angles :

(a) Constitutional

(b) Statutory

(c) Planning

(a) Constitutional

The Constitution of India under Article 243G empowered the tier of Panchayats to plan for items as devolved on to it. The intention of the Article is to have distinct devolution and distinct plan for each of the tiers of the Panchayats. However, the State Government is the deciding authority on such devolution.The items for planning for the Panchayats in the aggregate, as per Eleventh Schedule, are the following:

Items for Planning for Panchayats in Eleventh Schedule:

Sl. No *(1)*	*Eleventh Schedule* *(2)*
1.	Agriculture, including Agricultural Extension
2.	Land improvement, implementation of land reforms, land consolidation and soil conservation

(Contd.)

(Contd. Table)

Sl. No (1)	*Eleventh Schedule* (2)
3.	Minor irrigation, water management and watershed development
4.	Animal husbandry, dairying and poultry
5.	Fisheries
6.	Social Forestry and Farm Forestry
7.	Minor forest produce
8.	Small Scale industries including food processing industries
9.	Khadi, village and cottage industries
10.	Rural Housing
11.	Drinking water
12.	Fuel and fodder
13.	Roads, culverts, bridges, ferries, waterways and other means of communication
14.	Rural electrification, including distribution of electricity
15.	Non-conventional energy sources
16.	Poverty alleviation programme
17.	Education including primary and secondary schools
18.	Technical training and vocational education
19.	Adult and non-formal education
20.	Libraries
21.	Cultural activities
22.	Markets and fairs
23.	Health and Sanitation including hospitals, primary health centres, and dispensaries
24.	Family Welfare
25.	Women and Child Development
26.	Social welfare including welfare of the handicapped and mentally retarded
27.	Welfare of the weaker sections and in particular of the Scheduled Castes and Scheduled Tribes
28.	Public Distribution System
29.	Maintenance of community assets

(b) Statutory:

The State Panchayat Act also requires its tiers of the Panchayats in different states to address distinct items and plan for the same. In case the State Act has enacted devolution specific functional items, the planning items for the Panchayats would be distinct and confusion-free and meet the constitutional requirement as well. In some State Acts, there is provision for discretionary functions which are linked with historical role of Panchayats in the rural area. Such functional items, as are relevant at present, might be addressed in course of planning as well. In view of varying status of devolution, Panchayat Plans in general are bound to be different from one State to another and so also from one tier to another in particular. In that sense, the comparing plans among the Gram Panchayats, Block Panchayats and Zilla Panchayats among the States of India would not be possible. This is a big area of institutional reforms. Admitting the diversity of the country and the plural status of the growth of the Panchayats, a set of common programmes for each of the tiers of Panchayats might have been of immense help to develop a national character of the Panchayati system in the country. A model for devolution among the tiers of the Panchayats is an important area for institutional reform.

(c) Planning Agenda

The items for planning are varied but may be grouped as below:

(i) Planning for Devolved Programmes/Schemes

Planning for devolved items is the task set for Planning for the levels of Panchayats under Article 243G. Based on devolution of functional items out of the Eleventh Schedule, as enacted by the legislature of a state, the related tier of the Panchayat is required to take up planning for those items only. This is the defined area of constitutional responsibility for planning for any given tier in a state. From a constitutional angle, there is no other area where a tier of Panchayat may require to engage itself in plan related activities. In otherwords, planning for items beyond devolution does not fall under constitutional responsibility; it may as best be termed as institutional role of planning for a tier of Panchayat for such non-devolved items. Those may, however, to be planned.

(ii) Planning for assigned Programmes/schemes

In majority of States, as of now, tier specific devolution has not taken place. In such situation, a diluted version of devolution has been put in place by way of assignment of schemes in favour of tiers of Panchayats. Such tiers of Panchayats are assigned to execute a number of schemes along with tied-up funds on a regular basis e.g. NAREGA, BRGF etc. The related tier of Panchayats is required to plan for them.

(iii) Items suggested for planning in the 'Planning at the Grassroots Level'

'Planning at the Grassroots Level', as referred earlier, also dwelt on items which need to be captured under the Eleventh Five Year Plan or under the Annual Plan at the level of Panchayats. It has suggested to include following items for planning :

Gram Panchayat Plan

(1) The Anti Poverty Programme
(2) The Gender Justice Programme
(3) The Special Component and Tribal Programme
(4) Programmes for Social Security

Block Panchayat Plan

'Planning at the Grassroots Level' did not suggest separate items for the Block Panchayat Plan but mentioned that it would depend on the Activity Mapping for the Block Panchayat. It has suggested that the Intermediate Panchayat needs to address the following items as well :

(i) inter village-Panchayat issues
(ii) synergize inter-tier coordination for watershed development and Rural Business
(iii) inter-village road formation and multi-panchayat irrigation structures.

District Panchayat Plan

'Planning at the Grassroots Level' did not suggest separate items for the Zilla Panchayat Plan as well but mentioned again that items for planning would depend on Activity Mapping for the Zilla Panchayat. It has suggested that that the Zilla Panchayat needs to address the following:

(i) Gender Issues
(ii) Tribal Sub-plan
(iii) Special Component Plan for SCs

Further it has suggested that, based on subsidiarity principle, it may take up planning activities on the following areas as well:

(a) Agricultural land related issues
(b) Forest land related issues
(c) Credit and Usury related issues
(d) Livelihood related issues
(e) Primary Health Care and Nutrition Issues

Planning at the Grassroots Level' has not addressed tier specific functional items for the Panchayats but left it to be determined by the related State Government based on Activity Mapping. Incidentally, at para c) Devolution and clarity on devolution at chapter -4, the relevance of Activity Mapping vis-a-vis Functional Mapping has been discussed in details. Further, the role of upper tier of Panchayats as a supervisory body over lower tier of panchayats, as suggested, is not in tune with the spirit of Article 243G of the Constitution. Items for planning for each of the tiers of Panchayats need to be distinct and confusion-free. There has to exist no overlapping jurisdiction in between them.

(iv) Items included under the Flagship Programmes including Bharat Nirman

Among the various programmes being implemented in the country, eight programmes have been short listed as Flagship programmes to give focussed attention for its crucial role in the economy. These Programmes are intended to bring about economic and social sector transformation of our country. Those are as below:

1. National Rural Employment Guarantee Scheme
2. Sarva shiksha Abhiyan
3. Mid day Meal Scheme
4. Integrated Child Development Services (ICDS)
5. National Rural Health Mission (NRHM)
6. Jawaharlal Nehru National Urban Renewal Mission (JNNURM)
7. Total Sanitation Campaign (TSC)
8. Bharat Nirman
   - (i) Rural Roads
   - (ii) Rural Housing
   - (iii) Rural Drinking Water Supply
   - (iv) Irrigation
   - (v) Rural Electrification
   - (vi) Rural Telephony

It would appear that except JNNURM, most of the flagship programmes have been designed for rural areas. Regarding the Bharat Nirman programme it has been initiated to upgrade rural infrastructure in a time bound manner and have been discussed separately hereunder. All schemes taken up under the Flagship programme have dedicated funding support. Implementation of Flagship programmes, including Bharat Nirman programmes, is the joint responsibility of the ministries of the Government of India, departments of the State Government and for all tiers of Panchayats and Municipalities. The specific role of the tiers of Panchayats would vary from one State to another in relation to the status of devolution or of assignment of functions. The planning role of the tier of

Panchayats in Flagship Programme would accordingly vary. Thus, though no pattern is yet to emerge as distinct functional role of any tier of the Panchayats on the Flagship Programme, it would be worthwhile to mention that the core objective of each of the components of Flagship Programme need to be given appropriate attention while designing tier-specific Panchayat Plan. Even for similar nature of schemes out of its own resources the same spirit of the Flagship programme need to be followed.

Bharat Nirman

Bharat Nirman, as earlier mentioned, is a flagship programme launched by the Central Government in partnership with State Governments and Panchayat Raj Institutions to upgrade rural infrastructure in the country in a time bound manner. There are six components of this programme, as indicated earlier. While the agenda is not new, the effort here is to impart a sense of urgency to these goals. These investments in rural infrastructure will unlock the growth potential of our country.

The tasks undertaken under the programme are as follows:

- Every village to be provided electricity
- Every habitation of over 1000 population (500 in hilly and tribal areas) to be provided an all-weather road
- Every habitation to have a safe source of drinking water. In addition, all habitations which have slipped back from full coverage to partial coverage due to failure of sourcc, and habitations which have water quality problems to be addressed
- Every village to be connected by telephone
- Additional irrigation capacity to be created
- More houses to be constructed for the rural poor.

The planning role of the tiers of the Panchayats, as earlier pointed out, commences when any scheme on the aforesaid area is assigned to any tier of the Panchayat. At the time of formulation of the Annual Plan, it has to be planned properly and implemented efficiently. In case where any State

Government decides to implement all or part of such programmes by its line departments (telephone connectivity being the responsibility of the Central Government), the tiers of the Panchayats need to interact with such departments and ask to address the areas of deficit in its jurisdiction.

(v) Other Statutory Acts having linkage with Planning

As a general principle, the State Panchayat Act is the only Statute which the Panchayats at various levels need to follow for programme planning or otherwise. The planning solution of any current problem-either social or economic-has to be addressed within the limits of the State Panchayat Act. However, the publication of new Acts, whether Central or State, enjoins responsibility upon the tier of Panchayats to take action on them if found relevant in the planning front.

Three legislations may be mentioned in this context which have a bearing on Right-based approach on economic and social development and have to be comprehensively addressed at the time of planning itself.

(i) Mahatma Gandhi National Employment Guarantee Act, 2005

(ii) Right of Children to Free and Compulsory Education Act, 2009

(iii) The National Food Security Bill(likely to be enacted soon)

As to the National Employment Guarantee Act, the focal point for implementation has been vested with the Gram Panchayat. It is also the planning and implementing authority for schemes taken up in furtherance of the NREGA. Right of children to Free and Compulsory Education Act, 2009 has focused role of the institution of the Panchayat in general. The distinct role and functional responsibility of the tiers of Panchayats would depend on devolution or assignment of functions based on the principle of subsidiarity. The planning component of any action, if any, need to be appropriately covered by the tier of the Panchayats. Similarly, it is incumbent to spell out in clear terms the role of particular tier of Panchayat in respect of the proposed legislation on Food Security.

(vi) Millennium Development Goals, State Human Development Report and District Human Development Report

The Millennium Development Goals (MDGs) are an agreed set of goals and also objectives that international community set for itself at the UN Millennium Summit 2000. The underlying objective of the high-valued MDG declaration has been to ensure that human beings across the World have a bare minimum dignified level of living. The developed and the developing segments of this world would jointly address this area as partners. The developing countries would require revisiting their priorities on poverty eradication, health and education while the developed countries would be pledging their support through aid, debt relief and fairer trade. It has been envisaged that MDG Goals are not mere development objectives, it encompasses universally accepted human values and rights such as freedom from hunger, the right to basic education, the right to health and a responsibility to future generations.

The Millennium Development Goals (MDGs), as set for implementation and monitoring, are as follows:

Goal 1: Eradicate extreme poverty and hunger

Goal 2: Achieve universal primary education

Goal 3: Promote gender equality and empower women

Goal 4: Reduce child mortality

Goal 5: Improve maternal health

Goal 6: Combat HIV/AIDS, malaria and other diseases

Goal 7: Ensure environmental sustainability

Goal 8: Develop a global partnership for development

Based on MDG, the National Government, State Governments, Panchayats and Municipalities are addressing the subjects that fall under their jurisdiction and responsibility to reach the national targets in time. Findings of State Human Development Report or District Human Development Report usually reveal dissimilar status of human development across the Panchayats. Varying degree of planning efforts would be needed at the levels of the Panchayat to reach the goals of MDG.

(vii) **BRGF, PMGSY, RKVY etc and its linkage with the planning of the Panchayats**

The Ministries of Rural Development, Panchayat and Agriculture have respectively taken up very important schemes of the related Ministry like those of the flagship schemes of the Central Government. The guidelines on BRGF and RKVY have set in motion separate and parallel planning exercise. Separate Planning Processes do not appear to be well connected either with the timelines or with the annual planning exercise of the Gram Panchayat Plan, Block Panchayat Plan and Zilla Panchayat Plan. Such guidelines have brought in complication in the planning arena. The vision of the Panchayats at various levels, the stock taking exercise, infrastructural deficit and gaps, etc are to be the basis of plan formulation; such data should also be the common basis for BRGF and RKVY planning. The separate guidelines on BRGF and RKVY require the repeat of the same exercise from the angles of BRGF or RKVY and it strikes at the very sanctity of annual planning exercise at the levels of Panchayats. In any case, efforts to avoid duplicating exercises have to put in place and synchronise it with the annual planning exercises of the tiers of the Panchayat and treat funds under BRGF, RKVY, etc. as tied resources for its schemes. This would put at rest all confusions emanating from separate planning exercise on BRGF, etc., and clear all confusions between Plan, Plan of Action or Action Plan. The BRGF or RKVY is indeed very much a part of programmes under infrastructure, livelihood or agricultural plan of either under the GP Plan, the BP Plan or the ZP Plan. Once such plan has been settled at the appropriate level, the Action Plan on such items requires to be worked out just like DPR. This is true for BRGF or RKVY. In the context of current status of devolution, it is desirable that clear cut functional role of the respective tier of Panchayats is notified. The following areas need to be addressed for proper planning for BRGF, RKVY, etc :

(i) Determination of functional role of such schemes in between the lines departments of the State Government and the Panchayats at various levels namely, Gram Panchayat, Block Panchayat and Zilla Panchayat. In the event such items of works have not been formally devolved on to the tiers of Panchayat, the implementation task for relevant works has to be assigned to them.

(ii) It has now become a practice that DPR on BRGF or RKVY is prepared by a Consultant centrally for a district. The DPR so prepared for the BRGF or the RKVY need to be broken down for the related Gram Panchayats, Block Panchayats and Zilla Panchayat and then pose the same to the related tier of Panchayats for taking decision on its Annual plan.

(iii) Fund involvement for the respective unit of Panchayats has also to be simultaneously informed.

(iv) Based on scheme mapping (i.e. schemes of line departments, of Panchayats and of others) on the given area and having regard to spatial considerations, the concerned tier of Panchayat would be in a position to take decision on inclusion of them as its own schemes in the Annual Plan.

(viii) **Mission Mode Programmes**

The Government of India has launched a number of Mission mode programmes in the country with bagful of resources to address deficit, unmet needs and gaps in the crucial sectors having enough growth potentialities. Most of such programmes are connected with rural areas and have significant bearing in local level planning. Just like BRGF and RKVY, these programmes are, by and large, implemented by the line departments of the State Government. Even in cases where such programmes are implemented by the line departments of the State Governments, there are components which normally fall on the devolved responsibility of a particular tier of

Panchayats. Moreover, the tiers of Panchayats need to know the kind of other schemes being implemented in its given spatial area for preventing its duplication. This is also an area to tie-up possible forward or backward linkage. The Government of India has so far taken the following Mission mode programmes:

(i) National Food Security Mission
(ii) National Mission for Sustainable Agriculture
(iii) National Horticulture Mission
(iv) National Bamboo Mission
(v) Technical Mission on Oilseeds, Pulses & Maize
(vi) National Rural Health Mission
(vii) Mission Mode Projects under NeGP
(viii) Skilled development Mission
(ix) National Rural Livelihood Mission

Incidentally, it would be worth mentioning that role clarity of the tiers of Panchayats in all mission mode programmes including National Rural Livelihood Mission is urgently called for. Further, load bearing and organisational capacity of the related tier of the Panchayat deserves to be factored in before assigning one scheme after another to any tier of the Panchayats. Intervention in capacity development alone may not be good enough to ensure outreach, output and final outcome.

Selection of Schemes for the Annual Plan

The tier of Panchayats are thus faced with a number of choices and options to select from various considerations. One of the ways is to get feedback from Gram Sabha falling within a particular Gram Panchayat area. A Gram Sabha connects the citizens' felt-need with possible choice of schemes. However, for a Gram Sabha to be really useful and meaningful forum to sensor public perception of priorities, it is required to have a mechanism to know availability of schemes along with its fund entitlement for exercising their informed choice. The other considerations for selecting and formulating schemes would be to meet its constitutional duty to plan for devolved functions and also to those assigned to it with focus on human development and inclusive growth.

Matching Resources to Plan

A Plan is functionally meaningful when its schemes are backed up with required resources. There could be broadly two categories of schemes: having purely tied funds (in case of assigned schemes) and Purely untied funds (for own resources based schemes). For resources (grants) obtained on recommendations of State Finance Commission (for devolved schemes) or Central Finance Commission(for general purpose schemes) the funds are usually of the untied type. However, some grants may be tied (for specific schemes) as well. In States where centrally sponsored schemes are implemented by a particular tier of Panchayat, share of Central or the State Government also falls under tied category. Incidentally, since all schemes are to be audited by the office of the Accountant General, the mixing of tied funds with untied funds would attract serious audit objections on grounds of financial propriety. In cases where the tied fund is inadequate to address the felt needs of an area, a separate scheme (Part B) may be prepared with untied funds for the remaining area.

Once the needs and the corresponding scheme are settled, the corresponding source of funding have to be indicated in a summary statement to ensure that supporting funds for Planned schemes have been provided in the following manner.

Step 1 : Classifying each need into a matrix

Felt needs including human development needs as finally settled by the related unit of a tier of Panchayats require to be classified under broad headings.

Step 2 : Specifying Schemes against such classified needs

Schemes finally selected have to be indicated against corresponding needs.

Step 3 : Indicating nature of fund against such schemes

The nature of fund, tied or untied, and its possible allocation have to be shown against schemes so selected.

Presentation of Panchayat Plan

The 'Planning at the Grassroots Level' or the Manual on District Planning has not provided any format for presentation of Panchayat Plan. The guidelines issued by the Planning Commission at the time of formulation of the Eleventh Five Year Plan did not also prescribe any format for presentation of the Panchayat Plan. However, for the State Annual Plan, there are dedicated formats for presentation of Rural Local Body Plans (GNC-I) and Urban Local Body Plans (GNC-II). The said formats are based on heads of development. It is implied, there from, that formats for presentations of the tiers of Panchayats would also be modelled on heads of development. Additionally, since the District Annual Plans would be prepared by consolidating District Panchayats Plan and District Urban Body Plan, it would be necessary to have uniform framework of presentation of Annual Plan for proper consolidation. Accordingly, identical formats for presentation of Gram Panchayat Plan, Block Panchayat Plan and Zilla Panchayat Plan are necessary. A model is worked out here for having no approved format for presentation of Plan, as indicated in Tables AI, AII, AIII.

Note-The Format has to be prepared carefully. The Format has itself contained heads of development and it has to be retained as it is Columns relating to plan proposals are most important. Here Continuing Schemes mean those schemes which have been taken up in earlier plan period but could not be completed and that additional funds have to be made for the next year to complete the same. The name of the Continuing Scheme has to be written first and then the proposed outlay has to be indicated below in the same column. In case such schemes do not exist, it would be marked nil or 0 (zero). New schemes are meant those which are intended to be taken up for the proposed Annual Plan. Here again, the name of the scheme should be written first and then the

FORMATS FOR PRESENTATION OF PANCHAYAT PLANS (BASED ON THE 11TH SCHEDULE)

Format-A.I for Gram Panchayat Plan

Annual Plan-(say) 2011-12

Name of the Gram Panchayat———

Sector	*Major Heads of Development*	*Minor Heads of Development*	*Corresponding Items under 11th Schedule in bracket*	*Plan Proposals for 2011-12 (Rs in thousand)*		
				Continuing Schemes	*New Schemes*	*Total*
I	Agriculture and Allied Services	(a) Crop husbandry (b) Soil and water conservation (c) Animal husbandry and Dairy development (d) Fisheries (e) Other Agricultural Programme-Others Marketing and Quality Control	Agriculture, including agricultural extension (1); Soil Conservation (2), Animal husbandry, dairying and poultry (4), Fisheries (5), Fuel and fodder (12), Markets and fairs (22)			

(Contd.)

(Contd. Table)

Sector	*Major Heads of Development*	*Minor Heads of Development*	*Corresponding Items under 11th Schedule in Bracket*	*Plan Proposals for 2011-12 (Rs in thousand)*		
				Continuing Schemes	*New Schemes*	*Total*
II	Rural Development	(a) Land reforms, (b) Rural Employment	Land improvement, implementation of land reforms, land consolidation (2), Poverty alleviation programme (16)			
IV	Irrigation & Flood control/Minor Irrigation	Minor Irrigation	Minor irrigation,water management and wasteland development (3)			
V	Energy	(a) Integrated Rural Energy Programme (b) Nonconventional sources of Energy	Rural Electrification, including distribution of energy (14), Non-conventional Energy Sources (15)			

(Contd.)

(Contd. Table)

Sector	*Major Heads of Development*	*Minor Heads of Development*	*Corresponding Items under 11th Schedule in bracket*	*Plan Proposals for 2011-12 (Rs in thousand)*		
				Continuing Schemes	*New Schemes*	*Total*
VI	Industry and Minerals	Village and Small Enterprises	Small scale industries, including food processing industries (8), Khadi, village and cottage industries (9)			
VII	Transport	(a) Roads and Bridges (b) Other Transport Services	Roads, culverts, bridges ,ferries, waterways and other means of communication (13)			

(Contd.)

(Contd. Table)

Sector	*Major Heads of Development*	*Minor Heads of Development*	*Corresponding Items under 11th Schedule in Bracket*	*Plan Proposals for 2011-12 (Rs in thousand)*		
				Continuing Schemes	*New Schemes*	*Total*
VIII	Science, Technology and Environment	Forestry and wild life	Social forestry and farm forestry (6), Minor forest produce (7)			
IX	General Economic Services/Civil Service	Civil Supplies	Public distribution system (28)			

(Contd.)

(Contd. Table)

Sector	*Major Heads of Development*	*Minor Heads of Development*	*Corresponding Items under 11th Schedule in bracket*	*Plan Proposals for 2011-12 (Rs in thousand)*		
				Continuing Schemes	*New Schemes*	*Total*
X	Social Service	(a) Housing-Rural Housing(IAY) (b) General Education- (i) Elementary Education, (ii) Literacy/Adult Education (iii) Art and Culture (c) Technical Education (d) Medical and Public Health (e) Empowerment of Women and Development of Children	Rural Housing(10),Drinking Water(11), Education, including primary and secondary school (17), Technical training and vocational education (18), Adult and nonformal education (19), Libraries (20), Cultural activities (21), Health and Sanitation, including hospitals, primary health centres and dispensaries			

(Contd.)

(Contd. Table)

Sector	*Major Heads of Development*	*Minor Heads of Development*	*Corresponding Items under 11th Schedule in bracket*	*Plan Proposals for 2011-12 (Rs in thousand)*		
				Continuing Schemes	*New Schemes*	*Total*
		(f) Social Security and Social welfare of the handicapped (g) Develoment of SCs, STs and OBCs	(23), Family welfare (24), Women and child development (25), Social welfare, including welfare of the handicapped and mentally retarded (26), Welfare of the weaker sections, and in particular, of the Scheduled Castes and Scheduled Tribes (27)			
XI	Social Service	Non-Plan	*Maintenances of Community assets (29)			

*Non- Plan items need not come under Annual Plan

FORMAT-A.II FOR BLOCK PANCHAYAT PLAN ANNUAL PLAN-(SAY) 2011-12

Name of the Block Panchayat——

Sector	*Major Heads of Development*	*Minor Heads of Development*	*Corresponding Items under 11th Schedule in Bracket*	*Plan Proposals for 2011-12 (Rs in thousand)*		
				Continuing Schemes	*New Schemes*	*Total*
I	Agriculture and Allied Services	(a) Crop husbandry (b) Soil and water conservation (c) Animal husbandry and Dairy development (d) Fisheries (e) Other Agricultural Programme-Others Marketing and Quality Control	Agriculture, including (1) agricultural extension (2); Soil Conservation (3), Animal husbandry, dairying and poultry (4), Fisheries (5), Fuel and fodder (12), (6) Markets and fairs (22)			
II	Rural Development	(a) Land reforms, (b) Rural Employment	Land improvement, implementation of land reforms, land consolidation (2), Poverty alleviation programme (16)			

(Contd.)

(Contd. Table)

Sector	*Major Heads of Development*	*Minor Heads of Development*	*Corresponding Items under 11th Schedule in Bracket*	*Plan Proposals for 2011-12 (Rs in thousand)*		
				Continuing Schemes	*New Schemes*	*Total*
IV	Irrigation& Flood control/Minor Irrigation	Minor Irrigation	Minor irrigation,water management and wasteland development (3)			
V	Energy	(a) Integrated Rural Energy Programme (b) Nonconventional sources of Energy	Rural Electrification, including distribution of energy (14), Non-conventional Energy Sources (15)			
VI	Industry and Minerals	Village and Small Enterprises	Small scale industries, including food processing industries (8), Khadi, village and cottage industries (9)			

(Contd.)

(Contd. Table)

Sector	Major Heads of Development	Minor Heads of Development	Corresponding Items under 11th Schedule in Bracket	Plan Proposals for 2011-12 (Rs in thousand)		
				Continuing Schemes	New Schemes	Total
VII	Transport	a)Roads and Bridges b)Other Transport Services	Roads, culverts, bridges, ferries, waterways and other means of communication (13)			
VIII	Science, Technology and Environment	Forestry and wild life	Social forestry and farm forestry (6), Minor forest produce (7)			
IX	General Economic Services/Civil Service	Civil Supplies	Public distribution system (28)			

(Contd.)

(Contd. Table)

Sector	Major Head Of Development	Minor Heads of Development	Corresponding Items under 11th Schedule in bracket	Plan Proposals for 2011-12 (Rs in thousand)		
				Continuing Schemes	New Schemes	Total
X	Social Service	(a) Housing-Rural Housing(IAY) (b) General Education- (i) Elementary Education, (ii) Literacy/Adult Education (iii) Art&Culture (c) Technical Education (d) Medical & Public Health (e) Empowerment of Women & Development of Children (f) Social Security & Social Welfare of the handicapped	Rural Housing (10), Drinking Water (11), Education, including primary and secondary school (17), Technical training and vocational education (18), Adult and nonformal education (19), Libraries (20), Cultural activities (21), Health and Sanitation, including hospitals, primary health centres and dispensaries (23), Family			

(Contd.)

(Contd. Table)

Sector	*Major Head Of Development*	*Minor Heads of Development*	*Corresponding Items under 11th Schedule in bracket*	*Plan Proposals for 2011-12 (Rs in thousand)*		
		(g) Develoment of SCs, STs & OBCs	Welfare (24), Women and child development (25), Social welfare, including welfare of the handicapped and mentally retarded (26), Welfare of the weaker sections, and in particular, of the Scheduled Castes and Scheduled Tribes (27)			
XI	Social Service	Non-Plan	*Maintenances of Community assets (29)			

*Non- Plan items need not come under Annual Plan

PRESENTATION OF ZILLA PANCHAYAT PLAN
FORMAT- AIII
(for presentation of draft Zilla Panchayat Plan based on the 11th Schedule)
Annual Plan (may) 2011-12.......

Name of the Municipality.....

Sector	*Major Heads of Development*	*Minor Heads of Development*	*Corresponding Items under 11th Schedule in Bracket*	*Plan Proposals for 2011-12 (Rs in thousand)*		
				Continuing Schemes	*New Schemes*	*Total*
I	Agriculture and Allied Services	(a) Crop husbandry (b) Soil and water conservation (c) Animal husbandry and Dairy development (d) Fisheries (e) Other Agricultural Programme-Others Marketing and Quality Control	Agriculture, including agricultural extension(1); Soil Conservation(2), Animal husbandry, dairying and poultry (4), Fisheries (5), Fuel and fodder (12), Markets and fairs (22)			
II	Rural Development	(a) Land reforms, (b) Rural Employment	Land improvement, implementation of land reforms, land consolidation (2), Poverty alleviation programme (16)			

(Contd.)

(Contd. Table)

Sector	*Major Heads of Development*	*Minor Heads of Development*	*Corresponding Items under 11th Schedule in bracket*	*Plan Proposals for 2011-12 (Rs in thousand)*		
				Continuing Schemes	*New Schemes*	*Total*
III	Irrigation and Flood control/Minor Irrigation	Minor Irrigation	Minor irrigation, water management and wasteland development (3)			
IV	Energy	(a) Integrated Rural Energy Programme (b) Nonconventional sources of Energy	Rural Electrification, including distribution of energy (14), Non-conventional Energy Sources (15)			
V	Industry and Minerals	Village and Small Enterprises	Small scale industries, including food processing industries (8), Khadi, village and cottage industries (9)			

(Contd.)

(Contd. Table)

Sector	*Major Heads of Development*	*Minor Heads of Development*	*Corresponding Items under 11th Schedule in bracket*	*Plan Proposals for 2011-12 (Rs in thousand)*		
				Continuing Schemes	*New Schemes*	*Total*
VI	Transport	(a) Roads and Bridges (b) Other Transport Services	Roads, culverts, bridges, ferries, waterways and other means of communication (13)			
VII	Science, Technology and Environment	Forestry and wild life	Social forestry and farm forestry (6), Minor forest produce (7)			
VIII	General Economic Services/Civil Service	Civil Supplies	Public distribution system (28)			

(Contd.)

(Contd. Table)

Sector	Major Heads of Development	Minor Heads of Development	Corresponding Items under 11th Schedule in bracket	Plan Proposals for 2011-12 (Rs in thousand)		
				Continuing Schemes	New Schemes	Total
IX	Social Service	(a) Housing-Rural Housing (IAY) (b) General Education-I (i) Elementary Education, (ii) Literacy/ Adult Education (iii) Art and Culture (c) Technical Education (d) Medical and Public Health	Rural Housing (10), Drinking Water (11), Education, incuding primary and secondary school (17),Technical training and vocational education(18), Adult and nonformal education (19), Libraries (20), Cultural activities (21),Health and Sanitation, including hospitals, primary health centres and dispensaries (23), Family welfare (24),Women and child development (25), Social welfare			

(Contd.)

(Contd. Table)

Sector	*Major Heads of Development*	*Minor Heads of Development*	*Corresponding Items under 11th Schedule in bracket*	*Plan Proposals for 2011-12 (Rs in thousand)*		
		(e) Empowerment of Women and Development of Children (f) Social Security and Social welfare of the handicapped (g)Develoment of SCs, STs and OBCs	including welfare of the handicapped and mentally retarded (26), Welfare of the weaker sections, and in particular, of the Scheduled Castes and Scheduled Tribes (27)			
X	Social Service	Non-Plan	* Maintenances of Community assets (29)			

*Non- Plan items need not come under Annual Plan

proposed outlay has to be indicated below in the same column. All schemes falling under a minor head have to be serially numbered and then add them in the next column to indicate minor head-wise proposed outlay for the Annual Plan.

Depending on nature of devolution, it is certain that some of the minor heads of development may remain blank or nil for any tier of Panchayat. Further, it is also possible that among the same tier of Panchayat, there would be variation on plan priorities and so in its sectoral allocation.

Summary Statement

After all the units of the tiers of Panchayats have worked out their Formats (AI, AII and AIII) respectively, a summarised Statement has to be worked out from the same format with reference to major heads of development in GNC-I and send it to the DPC.

GNC-I : Summary of Annual Plan-2011-12-Proposed Outlay for —

(Rs in thousand)

(mention the name of GP or BP or ZP, as applicable)

Sector	*Major Heads of Developments*	*Proposed Outlay for 2011-12*
I	Agriculture and Allied Services	
III	Rural Development	
IV	Irrigation and Flood control/Minor Irrigation	
V	Energy	
VI	Industry and Minerals	
VII	Transport	
VIII	Science, Technology and Environment	
X	Social Service	
Total		

Scheme of funding Annual Plan,—(year)

A Statement on back-up Financial Resources for the Annual Plan—(Year) indicating there in the name of the

Panchayat body has to be attached, as below, to enable the DPC to ensure that due consideration has been given on availability of resources against plan proposals.

Name of the Panchayat body—, Annual Plan (Year)—

(a) Projected Resources for Devolved Programmes:

1. Projected Revenue available from own sources————

2. Grant available on recommendations from the State Finance Commission on devolved items————

3. Grant available on recommendations from Central Finance Commission on (mentioned) programme————

4. Other Grants receivable from the State Governments—

(b) Projected Resources for Assigned Programmes

5. Projected fund availability for:

(i) NAREGA

(ii) RKVY

(iii) BRGF

(iv) SSA

(v) Others(please specify)

(c) Projected Resources for Non- assigned programmes

(i) ——

(ii) ——

(d) Projected Resources from Financial Institutions for Programmes:

(i) ——

(ii) ——

(e) Projected Resources from Any Other Sources/ Institutions for Programmes:

(i) Gifts/Donations

(ii) Interest from any endowments

(f) Total Projected Fund Availability for the Annual Plan—— ———

(g) Total Plan Proposals for the Annual Plan——— -

6

Urban Planning by the Municipalities

Urban Scenario in Perspective

Out of India's total population of 1027 million as on 2001, about 742 million live in rural areas and 285 million in urban areas representing 62.8 and 27.8 percentage of the population respectively. There has taken place an increase of 2.1 percentage point of urban population in 2001 over 1991 census percentage of 25.7. The decadal growth of population in rural and urban areas during the same period is 17.9 and 31.2 percent respectively. The level of urbanisation in our country has not been uniform. Among the State and Union Territories, the National Capital Territory of Delhi is the most urbanised with 93% with urban population followed by Union Territory of Chadigarh (89.8%) and Tamil Nadu (66.6%). Among the major States, Tamil Nadu is the most urbanised State with 43.9% of population living in urban areas followed by Maharashtra (42.4%) and Gujrat (37.4%). The proportion of urban Population is the lowest in Himachal Pradesh with 9.8% followed by Bihar with 10.5%, Assam 12.7% and Orissa 14.9%. Further, in absolute number of persons living in the urban area, Maharashtra leads with 41million which is 14% of the total population in the country. Uttar Pradesh accounts for about 35 million followed by Tamil Nadu of 27 million. Additionally, the contribution of urban sector to GDP is estimated to be in the range of 50-60 percent.

The country has been undergoing rapid changes in its urban character. The number of municipalities has also been increasing by leaps and bounds in tandem with such changes. The population density, shortages of land space for development works, absence of land use plan, increasing demand for municipal services, the high expectation of quality of municipal services from educated urban population, relatively poor resource base and the Constitutional responsibility under the 74th Amendment have posed for new challenges for urban planning. Further, all municipal bodies are not of same size and same importance. While there are municipal corporations located in metropolitan cities, there are different types of municipalities located at state capital, district head quarter and Sub-divisional head quarter. Service demands for municipalities located at tourists spots and peri-urban areas are also different altogether. Besides, municipalities have been addressing non-plan nature of jobs till the other day and were really functioning as stand-alone local self government and acting as agency of the State Government. The new role of Municipalities as partners in the formulation of the District Plan has opened up new challenges. Hitherto Perspective Plan or Draft Development Plan has now to be segregated under Five Year Plan and Annual Plan. Based on physical features and environmental scenario, the Annual Plan is bound to be distinctly unique for each of the municipalities. However, there are common issues which have to be addressed by all the municipalities together. Such common issues are covered under the 12th Schedule of the Constitution as can be seen below:

Twelfth Schedule :

1. Urban Planning including town planning.
2. Regulation of land-use and construction of buildings.

3. Planning for economic and social development.
4. Roads and bridges.
5. Water supply for domestic, industrial and commercial purposes.
6. Public health, sanitation conservancy and solid waste management.
7. Fire services.
8. Urban forestry, protection of the environment and promotion of ecological aspects.
9. Safeguarding the interests of weaker sections of society, including the handicapped and mentally retarded.
10. Slum improvement and upgradation.
11. Urban poverty alleviation.
12. Provision of urban amenities and facilities such as parks, gardens, playgrounds.
13. Promotion of cultural, educational and aesthetic aspects.
14. Burials and burial grounds; cremations, cremation grounds and electric crematoriums.
15. Cattle pounds; prevention of cruelty to animals.
16. Vital statistics including registration of births and deaths.
17. Public amenities including street lighting, parking lots, bus stops and public conveniences.
18. Regulation of slaughter houses and tanneries.

The functional items under 12th Schedules have broadly two features: regulatory and developmental. The regulatory functions, which are broadly Nonplan in nature, include Regulation of land-use and construction of buildings (2), Prevention of cruelity to animals (15), Vital Statistics including registration of births and Deaths (16), Regulation of slaughter houses and tanneries (18). It is a fact that for performance of regulatory functions, infrastructural support is also required but those do not fall under core planning priorities of the municipal bodies. The core planning priorities of the municipal planning are for meeting development needs, including basic minimum needs of its citizens.

Be that as it may, the framework of common priority areas of planning of the Municipalities may be focused under the following heads:

(a) Infrastructure, Land Use and Environment Development

(b) Social and Livelihood Development

(c) Municipal Institutional Strengthening

The above broad groupings may be broken down under its functional components.

(a) Infrastructure, Land Use and Environment Development

(i) Infrastructure

Infrastructure is a broad term and covers a good number of items including Slum Infrastructure Improvement Plan, Intra-municipal Infrastructure Plan and Trans-municipal Infrastructure Plan. The Slum Infrastructure Improvement Plan is usually designed to address local slum specific Water Supply, Sanitation, Solid waste Management, Local Drainage, Access Roads, Connected Street Lighting and other social Infrastructure like health unit, primary school, community centre etc.

Intra-municipal Infrastructure Improvement also addresses in a different format and scale on Water Supply, Sanitation, Solid Waste Management, Area level storm water drainage, Roads, bridges and traffic management, Social Infrastructure like educational institutions, Play ground, recreational centres, health units, markets, public utilities and conveniences.

Trans-municipal Infrastructure includes water treatment and transmission, Treatment of sewerage, and area drainage, Solid waste disposal, Roads, bridges and traffic management and Social infrastructure.

(ii) Land Use Development Plan

The relevance of land use planning is its significance to absorb increasing pressure of urbanization. The purpose of land use planning is to regulate the use of land to prevent misuse, overuse and abuse of this resource. Thus, land use planning mainly aims at meeting the consumption needs of growing population through optimum utilisation of resources.

Land Use Development is forward looking and future shaping in character as it is connected with designing of the edifice and the elevation of the municipal town. It is centred on Zoning and identifying development areas for health care, education, recreation including parks and gardening and public utilities etc.

(iii) Environment Development

The Environment Management Plan is a very important area of municipal planning because of its close linkage with other sub-components. It is connected with public health and hygiene and its degradation affects the citizens at large specially the poor and the vulnerable groups. Its social cost is beyond any measurement. It is for the same reason that it is required to ensure ambient Air Quality including noise, prevent land contamination, protect Water quality of sources like streams, rivers, ponds and the lakes. It is required to preserve bio-diversity, as relevant and applicable within its urban limits, and protect and preserve Flora, Fauna, Green cover and other heritage structures.

The overarching planning objective is inspired by the fact that many of the environmental damages are of an irreversible nature and that Environment does not follow any administrative boundaries.

(b) Social and Livelihood Development

The increasing density of urban population accompanied by in-migration of the rural population and also of different types of daily commuters in urban areas, in search of livelihood and other options, has put on considerable pressure on social and livelihood options and its development. Bigger efforts are called for livelihood and other support system. Such support system can be grouped as below:

(i) Livelihood and Poverty Alleviation
(ii) Local Economic Development
(iii) Healthcare Services Delivery Improvement
(iv) Primary Education Development Plan

Livelihood and Poverty Alleviation

The traditional role of the urban local bodies did not have any functioning area on Livelihood. With the empowerment of the municipalities under the 12th Schedule and the emerging of sizable number of urban BPL population, the Livelihood and Poverty Alleviation planning has now assumed a focused programme for the municipality. However, in view of paucity of financial resources the municipalities do not take up such programmes of its own but implement the national or state sponsored programmes as assigned to them for the improvement of quality of life of BPL and other weaker sections of population. Modelled on NAREGA, the Central Government has designed a new urban poverty alleviation programme and the municipalities of the country are required to implement them with fund released through the State Government.

Local Economic Development

High rate of urban population growth combined with the inability of the formal sector to generate sufficient employment has led to the emergence of informal sector to absorb in significant way the urban workforce seeking alternative means of livelihood. The municipalities have social responsibility to intervene in meaningful way on this emerging area. Such intervention can be done by way of integrated approach on infrastructure, improved tools, appropriate machinery, innovations, credit linkage, training, EDP, marketing outlets and the like. The invaluable role of facilitator is the hall mark of planning in this area.

Health Care Services Delivery Improvement

Primary health care in urban areas has generally been looked upon as an extension of state health care system. For the same reason, with few exceptions, primary health care has never been considered as a part of municipal service delivery system. The realisation of crucial role of dedicated primary health care in urban areas together with constitutional empowerment on public health related activities requires the municipalities to take care on preventive aspects, like vector control, RCH and other Public Health Issues. The phenomenal growth of slum population in some wards of municipalities also calls for appropriate family welfare programme. Additionally, the area of programme partnership and shared health planning with Government functionaries and NGOS working in the municipal area is another important aspect of this planning area.

Primary Education Development Plan

Primary Education plays a crucial role in the social and economic integration of children into a city or a nation. Except under some heritage municipality, primary education has never been an integral part of the municipal service delivery system. In course of evaluation of SSA and other educational surveys, it appears that urban areas account for sizable percentage of drop-outs originating from low income families. Further, school environment in good number of schools are not student friendly at all in that there are glaring deficiencies on basic infrastructure, drinking water facility, sanitation facility and electricity. Addition to that is the inadequate availability of required teaching aids and other equipments. As a result the quality of teaching is not of expected level. With the introduction of Mid-day meal for primary schools in the urban areas also, the space constraint along with its actual supply of mid-day meal in time has been posing considerable problem in some of such schools. Education plan for the Municipality requires addressing these issues.

Municipal Institutional Strengthening

The Constitutional vision on the 74th Amendment requires the Municipalities to redesign and restructure its organisation and more particularly of its functioning behaviour to meet its new challenges along with its quality. Strengthening municipal governance is aimed to put in place such organisational preparedness. Such programme includes Organisational Development Plan (including training and capacity), Process and Systems improvement Plan, Citizen's Interface Plan and Financial Plan.

In short, the Municipal Plan has to make a balance of the following:

(i) Needs of various sectors
(ii) Needs of different stakeholders
(iii) Financial resources as identified and tied up
(iv) Organisational plan for implementation of schemes

Methodology of Urban Planning

The Methodology of Urban Planning would almost be similar to those followed in the rural areas for the tiers of the Panchayats. The methodology of planning for the Panchayats has been based on recommendations of the 'Planning at the Grassroots Level' published by the Ministry of Panchayats, Government of India. The said methodology was structured on high valued participatory planning for the design of prioritisation for the local level plans. That methodology-a kind of grammar for decentralised planning- need also to be followed, mutatis mutandis, in the formulation of Annual Plan for the urban local bodies as well. Those are reiterated as below:

Step-I : Participating in building District Vision and setting its linkage with Vision of the Municipality

It has been earlier mentioned that building the district vision is the first requirement of a Five Year Plan. The Municipalities are required to be actively involved in designing the District vision particularly its component on urban vision. Such vision is not to be developed and imposed by district level functionaries but be formed through an interactive process of participation of all stakeholders- the local bodies and civil societies at large- for its acceptance and ownership.

Normally such a vision would stay for a period of time, say 5- years, and that it may not lapse into a case of annual exercise. However, there is no bar if the said stakeholders meet on an annual basis to take stock of changing environment and update it accordingly.

The core Vision is not to be conditioned by schemes and programmes but would be primarily articulated in terms of goals and outcomes. It needs to address three aspects of development namely, human development indicator, infrastructure development and development in the productive sector. A vision on human development indicator needs to cover health, education, women and child welfare, social justice and availability of basic minimum services. The vision for infrastructure may be formed on the basis of the components of JNNURM and other mega projects while the vision for the productive sector needs to take into consideration the potentialities in the district and what can be reached within the vision period taking into consideration the natural and human resources available in the district.

Step -II Undertaking a Parallel Stock Taking Exercise

Paralleling the envisioning process, a stocktaking exercise is to be taken up on assessment of quality of life and the availability of natural, social and financial resources and infrastructure. The data so obtained could be put in a development radar, as used by the Planning Commission for preparing the National Human Development Report, 2001- a kind of pictorial description of the performance of a unit of planning in respect of health, education ,poverty alleviation, drinking water, housing etc.

Such stocktaking exercises need also to include physical and financial achievement of services provided by the Government and the Private Sector. Natural resources data base already available in the GIS system in the district need also to be made use of for the planning of the concerned municipality.

Step-III Knowing the Citizens

'Planning for whom' is an important issue that needs to be seriously discussed at the beginning of any planning exercise. With it is connected the inclusive development approach of any Municipality. The census figures give a broad overview of the structure of population which need to be further broken down in terms of children, adolescents, and the Aged. The number of physically and mentally challenged persons and the persons belonging to Schedule Castes, Schedule tribes and other Backward Castes have also to be kept on record together with the number of BPL of population. At the time of formulation of the Annual Plan, programmes for all of them should be included as far as possible.

In this connection it is worthwhile to note that urban management is directly linked with number of population and alarming growth is the positive threat on urban infrastructure and services. All the local bodies have national duty to ensure that overload of population burden does not jeopardise the entire service delivery system.

Step-IV : Meeting at Ward Sabha

The Municipalities are also required to consult Ward Committee/sabha as part of Constitutional duty and compliance of Article 243S. Such consultation is also required to meet the needs of participatory planning and sensor the citizen's perception of felt-needs and its prioritisation.

Planning items for the Municipalities:

The planning items for the **Municipalities** would then need to be focused on three aspects:

(a) Constitutional

(b) Statutory

(c) Planning

It has earlier been mentioned that the items included in 12th Schedule and devolution of them by the State Government determine the functional boundary of the Municipalities.

Additionally, the Municipalities are required to perform certain duties which fall in their related State Act. Moreover, the Central Government or the State Government introduces new programmes meant for urban areas where the Municipalities happen to act as planning and implementing authorities. Appropriate address on all these areas have to be made by such Municipalities. Additionally, relavant items as on Flagship Programmes and MDG would also be applicable here.

Step V : Classifying each Need into a Matrix and Specifying Schemes Against such Classified Needs

Felt needs including human development needs as finally settled by the Municipality require to be classified under broad heads and schemes finally selected have to be indicated against corresponding needs.

Step VI : Indicating Nature of Fund Against such Schemes

The nature of fund, tied or untied, and its possible allocation have to be shown against schemes so selected at Format B.

Note-The Format has to be prepared carefully. The Format has itself contained heads of development and it has to be retained as it is. Columns relating to plan proposals are most important. Here Continuing Schemes mean those schemes which have been taken up in earlier plan period but could not be completed and that additional funds have to be made for the next year to complete the same. The name of the Continuing scheme has to be written first and then the proposed outlay has to be indicated below in the same column. In case such schemes do not exist, it would be marked nil or 0 (zero). New schemes are meant those which are intended to be taken up for the proposed Annual Plan. Here again, the name of the scheme should be written first and then the proposed outlay has to be indicated below in the same column. All schemes falling under a minor head have to be serially numbered and then add them in the next column to indicate minor head wise proposed outlay for the Annual Plan.

PRESENTATION OF MUNICIPAL PLAN
FORMAT-B
(for presentation of draft Municipal Plan based on the 12th Schedule)
Annual Plan Year

Name of the Municipality.....

Sector	*Major Heads of Development*	*Minor Heads of Development*	*Corresponding Items under 12th Schedule*	*Plan Proposals for 2011-12 (Rs. in thousand)*		
				Continuing schemes	*New schemes*	*Total*
VII	Transport	Roads and bridges	Roads and bridges (4)			
VIII	Science, Technology and Environment	Ecology and Environment	Urban forestry, protection of the environment and promotion of ecological aspects (8)			
IX	General Economic Services	Other General Economic Services-District Planning/District Councils	Urban planning including town planning (1), Planning for economic and social development (3)			

(Contd.)

(Contd. Table)

Sector	*Major Heads of Development*	*Minor Head Of Development*	*Corresponding Items under 12th Schedule*	*Plan Proposals for 2011-12 (Rs. in thousand)*		
X	Social Service		Water Supply for domestic, industrial and commercial purposes (5), Public health, sanitation, conservancy and waste management (6), Fire Services (7), Safeguarding the interests of weaker sections of society, including the handicapped and mentally retarded (9), Slum improvement and up gradation (10), Urban proverty alleviation (11), Promotion of urban amenities and facilities such as parks, gardens and			

(Contd.)

(Contd. Table)

Sector	*Major Heads of Development*	*Minor Heads of Development*	*Corresponding Items under 12th Schedule*	*Plan Proposals for 2011-12 (Rs in thousand)*		
			Playground (12), Promotion of cultural, educational and aesthetic aspects (13), Burials and burial grounds and electric crematoriums (14), Cattle ponds (15), Public amenities including street lighting, parking lots, bus stops and public conveniences(17)			
	Social Service	*Non-Plan	Regulation of land-use and construction of buildings (2), Prevention of cruelty to animals (15),Vital Statistics including registration of births and Deaths (16), Regulation of slaughter houses and tanneries (18)			

Note :*Non- Plan items need not come under Annual Plan.

Depending on nature of devolution, it is certain that some of the minor heads of development may remain blank or nil for any Municipality. Further, it is also certain that there would be variation on plan priorities among the Municipalities and so also in its sectoral allocation.

Summary Statement

After the Municipalities have worked out their Format-B, a summarised Statement has to be worked out from the same format with reference to major heads of development in GNC-II and send it to the DPC.

GNC-II : Summary of Annual Plan-2011-12- Proposed Outlay for —(mention the name of Municipality)

(Rs in thousand)

Sector	*Major Heads of Developments*	*Proposed Outlay for 2011-12*
VII	Transport	
VIII	Science, Technology and Environment	
IX	General Economic Services	
X	Social Service	

The DPC would then add them up are prepare the GNC-II for the district. It would be the responsibility of the Planning Department of the State to prepare the GNC-II of the state after edting them up in the similar format.

Scheme of funding Annual Plan,—(year)

A Statement on back-up Financial Resources for the Annual Plan—(Year) indicating there in the name of the Municipality has to be attached, as below, to enable the DPC to ensure that due consideration has been given on availability of resources against plan proposals.

Name of the Municipality—, Annual Plan—

(a) Projected Resources for Devolved Programmes:

1. Projected Revenue available from own Sources————
2. Grant available on recommendations from the State Finance Commission on devolved items————
3. Grant available on recommendations from Central Finance Commission on (mentioned) programme———
4. Other Grants receivable from the State Governments—

(b) Projected Resources for Assigned Programmes

5. Projected fund availability from:

(i) JNNURM
(ii) UDISSIMT
(iii) UIDSET
(iv) Integrated Development of small and medium Town.
(v) Integrated Development in Megacities.
(vi) Urban Water Supply and Sanitation.
(vii) Nehru Rozgar Yojana
(viii) Urban Basic Services for the Poor (UBSP)
(ix) Environmental Improvment of Urban slums
(x) Prime Ministers Urban Poverty Eradication Programme
(xi) BRGF
(xii) SSA
(xiii) Others(please specify)

(c) Projected Resources for Non- assigned Programmes

(i) ——
(ii) ——

(d) Projected Resources from Financial Institutions for Programmes

(i) ——
(ii) ——

(e) Projected Resources from Any Other Sources/ Institutions for Programmes

(i) Gifts/Donations

(ii) Interest from any Endowments

(f) Total Projected Fund Availability for the Annual Plan——— ———

(g) Total Plan Proposals for the Annual Plan———

7

Consolidation of Rural and Urban Plans by the District Planning Committee

Consolidation denotes in ordinary vocabulary strengthening or reinforcing. It is also used to mean amalgamation, merger, combination, incorporation, union, etc. The economic meaning of consolidation is of combining several actions into one. Such meaning varies with its application areas e.g. consolidation of land holdings, consolidation of soil, consolidation of debt, consolidation of loan, consolidation of business, consolidation zones etc.

Consolidation in the context of a district plan, as per Constitution of India, means that the District Planning Committee is required to consolidate plans prepared by the Panchayats and the Municipalities in the district and prepare a draft development plan for the district as a whole. The Constitution of India did not define separately the meaning of consolidation of plan presumably because it did not want to bring in any new functional meaning on consolidation of plan other than its usual meaningful aggregation. The consolidation in this context never intended physical consolidation of programmes/ schemes since it is well nigh impossible to connect and consolidate discrete schemes of different descriptions located at varied spatial areas. Many of such schemes are stand-alone schemes and not even consolidation friendly.

Similarly, it did not define "draft development plan" possibly because it wanted to confer generic responsibility on planning in favour of the Panchayats and the Municipalities and generic role of consolidation to the DPC. Further, the adjective 'draft' has perhaps been retained to enable State Government to suggest views, if any and its appropriate accommodation at the time of approval of its Annual Plan by the respective local body as per statutory obligation under respective State Panchayat Act/State Municipal Act before initiating further action on budgetary sanction. Additionally, such generic empowerment gives flexibility to include all kinds of plan- (a) perspective development plan of the area, (b) a five year plan as a counterpart of the national and state level five year plan or (c) an annual plan again as a counterpart of the State annual plan. However, the methodology of Consolidation needs to be the same in all cases.

Before proceeding further on consolidation of plans, it is desirable that conceptual confusion surrounding this new area needs to be cleared and homogeneity in conceptual understanding be put in place. The plural views do not necessarily augur well either in fine-tuning its essence or in focusing its actionable areas. Ordinarily, the confusion related to consolidation springs from two core concepts-planning and plan. The planning denotes interactions with stakeholders and deciding on best possible choice among the available alternatives given the resource constraint and other stipulations. The document that embodies such decisions is known as plan. Now, planning is a unique function in respect of any local body. Based on objective reality, there might be variation of the outcome of planning exercise for any local body. The underlying feature of planning exercise remains, however, the same for all; it is process in character. It is a process through which planning priorities are settled. It is precisely for the same reason that it is just not possible to consolidate any process function- least of all the consolidation of planning functions of the Panchayats or the Municipalities. In fact, there cannot exist any concept like consolidation of planning and there is also no scope for any DPC to assume that role.

It is in this very context that the Constitution of India requires the DPC to consolidate plans prepared by the Panchayats and Municipalities. The consolidation here means aggregation of plans formulated by all the Panchayats (Gram Panchayats, Block Panchayats and Zilla Panchayat) and also all the Municipalities in the district.

For intelligent consolidation of any such plans, a meaningful medium is required. Such a meaningful medium already exists in the area of State Plan where, as per Planning Commission's guidelines, plan schemes of implementing departments of the State are to be presented as per its nature of development function under relevant heads of development - major head and minor head. If schemes of two or more plan implementing departments address a common development function, those are to be grouped under the common heads of development-major and minor. In the process, a kind of consolidation of such schemes within the said heads of development also takes place. Now, the same medium-heads of development-also holds good for consolidation of plans of the Panchayats and the Municipalities by the DPC. Such heads of development wise presentation is intelligent in nature and consolidation-friendly. It would facilitate smoother consolidation of the Rural Plan by way of capturing total investment of the tiers of Panchayat under the given heads of development. Similarly, it would make it easier to prepare the Urban Plan by way of capturing total investment of all the Municipalities in the district under the given heads of development. The same platform of heads of development would similarly help proper consolidation of Rural Plan and Urban Plan into Draft District

Plan. In other words, consolidation in the context of Draft Development Plan would mean consolidation of plans in financial terms only and that such plans have to be presented under heads of development concept of the Planning Commission on the annual plan format meant for the related local body.

Methodology of Working on Consolidation by the DPC:

The first stage for the consolidation process is to segregate Annual plan proposals, Panchayats-wise (i.e. Gram Panchayat wise, Block Panchayat wise and Zilla Panchayat wise) and Municipalities-wise. The plans received from the tiers of Panchayats would together constitute the Rural Plan or Panchayat Plan for the district while plans received from the Municipalities would determine Urban Plan or Municpal plan for the district. In preparing the Rural plan, it has to be ensured that all plans have since been received from Gram Panchayats, Block Panchayats and the Zilla Panchayat. Devolution of powers and responsibilities are distinct and different among the levels of Panchayats but are identical in respect of a particulare tier of the Panchayat Gram Panchayat or Block Panchayat or Zilla Panchayat. Accordingly, in preparing the Draft Rural plan, it would be desirable to consolidate separately first Gram Panchayat Plans, then Block Panchayat Plans and thereafter take up consolidation of all Gram Panchayat Plans, Block Panchayat Plans and Zilla Panchayat Plan into Draft District Rural Plan or the Draft District Panchayat Plan.

The second stage of consolidation is with reference to urban local bodies. In view, however, of uniform devolution of function and responsibilities among the municipalities, there would not have any variation on planning responsibilities and accordingly plans submitted by all the municipalities may be taken up at the same time for its consolidation into Draft District Urban Plan or the Draft District Municipal Plan.

The final stage of consolidation is the preparation of the Draft District Pan and has to be so done by consolidating the Draft Rural plan and Draft Urban plan.

The step by step approach by itself is not enough; for meaningful consolidation, some facilitating tool is required. The facilitating tool for consolidation is met by the specially designed Consolidation Sheets. Consolidation Sheet-1 is meant for Gram Panchayats' Plans, Consolidation Sheet-2 is meant for Block Panchayats' Plans, Consolidation Sheet-3 is to capture Zilla Panchayat Plan and Consolidation Sheet-4 is meant for Consolidation of all Gram+Block+Zilla Panchayat Plans. Similarly, separate Consolidation Sheet has been designed for Urban or Municipalities' Plans. So, Consolidation Sheet-5 is meant for consolidation of all Municipalities' Plans. Finally, Consolidation Sheet-6 is meant for consolidation of all Panchayats[Rural] Plans and Municipalities' [Urban] Plans into Draft District Plan. As mentioned earlier, Consolidation sheets have been designed in terms of sectors linked with heads of development concept of the Planing Commission and also only in financial terms.

Consolidation of Gram Panchayats Plans
- Consolidation Sheet-1

Consolidation Sheet-1 is for consolidation of all Gram Panchayats' Plans for the Annual Plan, 2011-12 in terms of sectors as included in plan proposals.

Consolidation of Block Panchayats Plans
- Consolidation Sheet-2

Consolidation Sheet-2 is for consolidation of all Block Panchayats' [BP] Plans for the Annual Plan, 2011-12 in terms of sectors as included in plan proposals

Consolidation of Zilla Panchayat Plan
- Consolidation Sheet-3

Consolidation Sheet-3 is the Statement of Zilla Panchayat Plan for the Annual Plan, 2011-12 in terms of sectors as included in plan proposals

- Consolidation Sheet-1

(Rs in thousands)

Name and Serial no of GP	*Projected Outlay of Sector-I*	*Projected Outlay of Sector-II*	*Projected Outlay of Sector-IV*	*Projected Outlay of Sector-V*	*Projected Outlay of Sector-VI*	*Projected Outlay of Sector-VII*	*Projected Outlay of Sector-VIII*	*Projected Outlay of Sector-IX*	*Projected Outlay of Sector-X*	*Total Projected Outlay for the Annual Plan*
GP-1										
GP-2										
...										
GP-N										
Total										

N=Last serial no of Gram Panchayats.

Total = indicates GP Plan for the District.

Consolidation Sheet-2

(Rs in thousands)

Name and Serial no of BP	*Projected Outlay of Sector-I*	*Projected Outlay of Sector-II*	*Projected Outlay of Sector-IV*	*Projected Outlay of Sector-V*	*Projected Outlay of Sector-VI*	*Projected Outlay of Sector-VII*	*Projected Outlay of Sector-VIII*	*Projected Outlay of Sector-IX*	*Projected Outlay of Sector-X*	*Total*
BP-1										
BP-2										
...										
GP-N										
Total										

N=Last serial no of Block Panchayats

Consolidation Sheet-3

(Rs in thousands)

Name of the Zilla Panchayat	*Projected Outlay of Sector-I*	*Projected Outlay of Sector-II*	*Projected Outlay of Sector-IV*	*Projected Outlay of Sector-V*	*Projected Outlay of Sector-VI*	*Projected Outlay of Sector-VII*	*Projected Outlay of Sector-VIII*	*Projected Outlay of Sector-IX*	*Projected Outlay of Sector-X*	*Total*
Total										

Consolidation Sheet-4

(Rs. in Thousands)

Sector (1)	*Consolidated Proposed Outlay of GPs* (2)	*Consolidated Proposed Outlay of BPs* (3)	*Proposed Outlay of ZP* (4)	*Total* (5)	*Cosolidated Proposal Sectorwise Outlay of the Panchayats for the Annual Plan* (6)
Sector-I					
Sector-II					
Sector-IV					
Sector-V					
Sector-VI					
Sector-VII					
Sector-VIII					
Sector-IX					
Sector-X					
Total					

Note : (a) Figure in column (5) and column (6) would be identical.
(b) Total in the last column and row indicates aggregate picture of Panchayat Plan in the district.

Consolidated picture of Rural Plan

GNC-I : Annual Plan-2011-12-Proposed Outlay (Rural Local Bodies)

(Rs in thousand)

Sector	*Major Heads of Developments*	*Proposed Outlays for 2011-12*
I	Agriculture and Allied Services	
II	Rural Development	
IV	Irrigation and Flood control/Minor Irrigation	
V	Energy	
VI	Industry and Minerals	
VII	Transport	
VIII	Science, Technology and Environment	
X	Social Service	
Total	All heads of developments	

Consolidation of Municipal Plans- Consolidation Sheet-5

(Rs in thousand)

Name and Serial no of Municipalities	*Projected Outlay of Sector-VII*	*Projected Outlay of Sector-VIII*	*Projected Outlay of Sector-IX*	*Projected Outlay of Sector-X*	*Total Projected outlay for the Annual Plan*
Municipality-1					
Municipality-2					
....					
Municipality-N					
Total					

N=Last serial no of Municipalities

Consolidated picture of Urban Plan

GNC-II : Annual Plan-2011-12-Proposed Outlay (Urban Local Bodies)

(Rs in thousand)

Sector	*Major Heads of Developments*	*Proposed Outlay for 2011-12*
VII	Transport	
VIII	Science, Technology and Environment	
IX	General Economic Services	
X	Social Service	

Total All heads of Development

Consolidation Sheet-6- draft District Plan

(Rs. in Thousands)

Local bodies (1)	*Consolidated Proposed Outlay of Sector-I* (2)	*Consolidated Proposed Outlay of Sector-II* (3)	*Consolidated Proposed Outlay of Sector-IV* (4)	*Consolidated Proposed Outlay of Sector-V* (5)	*Consolidated Proposed Outlay of Sector-VI* (6)
Panchayats (Rural)					
Municipalities (Urban)					
Total					

Local bodies	*Consolidated Proposed Outlay of Sector-VII* (7)	*Consolidated Proposed Outlay of Sector-VIII* (8)	*Consolidated Proposed Outlay of Sector-IX* (9)	*Consolidated Proposed Outlay of Sector-X* (10)	*Consolidated Proposed Outlay of Sector-XI* (11)	*Total* (12)
Panchayats (Rural)						
Municipalities (Urban)						
Total						

Note : Total at row 3 column 12 gives consolidated figure of the draft District Plan for the Annual Plan.

Consolidation of Gram+ Block+ Zilla Panchayat Plan-Consolidation Sheet-4

Consolidation Sheet-4 is for consolidation of all Gram+Block+Zilla Panchayats Plans for the Annual Plan 2011-12 in terms of sectors as included in plan proposals

Consolidated picture of Rural Plan

Based on Consolidation Sheet-4, the GNC-I format required by the Planning Commission for the proposed Annual Plan outlay of the State for Rural Local Bodies can be filled in easily.

Consolidation of Municipal Plans- Consolidation Sheet-5

Consolidation Sheet-5 is for consolidation of all Municipalities' Plans for the Annual Plan, 2011-12 in terms of sectors as included in plan proposals.

Consolidated picture of Urban Plan

Based on Consolidation Sheet-5, the GNC-II format required by the Planning Commission for the proposed Annual Plan outlay of the State for Urban Local Bodies can be filled in easily.

Consolidation of Rural+Urban Plan- Consolidation Sheet-6- draft District Plan

Consolidation Sheet-6 is for consolidation of all Panchayats[Rural] Plans and Municipalities'[Urban] Plans) for the Annual Plan,2011-12in terms of sectors as included in plan proposals and preparation of draft District Development Plan

8

Draft District Plans-the Role of the State Planning Board and the State Government

The Article 243ZD of the Constitution provides that every District Planning Committee shall prepare the Draft Development Plan and then forward the same to the Government of the State. The Constitution of India has not defined the Draft Development Plan nor has it mentioned the time when it has to be so forwarded or the follow-up role of the State Government in this regard. The role of the State Planning Board is also not expressly provided since the institution of the State Planning Board does not have any Constitutional existence. In some States e.g., in West Bengal, the State Government is required, in consultation with the State Planning Board and after giving the DPC an opportunity to present its plan, approve the plan with such modification as that Government deems fit.

The Constitutional authority in the forum of the State Government may either approve the District plans or send it back with its comments. In the true spirit of the Article 243ZD, it is desirable that the State Government may not formally undertake any exercise on approval but may accord certain comments based on objective assessments. The responsibility for giving comments may be delegated to the State Planning Board. A model check-list for scrutiny may be followed for processing comments on Draft District Plans, namely:

(a) On Substantive Part

(i) With Reference to Respective Devolved Items

The Constitution of India requires the State Governments to devolve distinct functional items of the Eleventh Schedule for each of the tiers of Panchayat in the State. Similarly, it requires functional items of the Twelfth Schedule to be devolved on to the municipalities. On the basis of such devolved items, the concerned local body is required to undertake planning exercise for the Five Year/Annual Plan. It is to be looked into whether the concerned local bodies have duly made plan on them.

(ii) With Reference to Assigned Scheme Schemes, if any

Gram Panchayats, Block Panchayats or Zilla Panchayat or Municipalities are very often assigned to execute certain national or state schemes. Some of such schemes also fall in the category of Flagship Programme of the country, namely, NAREGA or JNNURM, etc. Some other important schemes assigned to them include BRGF (Backward Scheme Grant Fund), RSVY (Rashtriya Sam Vikash Yojana), JSY (Janani Suraksha Yojana) etc. The funds in question of all such schemes are made available to local bodies for execution of schemes by the Central Government through the State Government. It has to be seen whether such assigned schemes have been incorporated under their respective plan and incorporated under resources.

(iii) With Reference to Actual Fund at their Disposal

No plan is of any substance unless it is backed up by matching fund. The culture of resource-based planning is not the hallmark of decentralised local bodies. As a matter of fact, it has yet to become a part of planning discipline and culture at the decentralised level. The plan of any local need not turn out to be a mere wish-list of schemes or a catalogue of schemes. The draft development plan needs to have resource-back up – both tied and untied. The scheme of financing a district plan has to be an essential item of scrutiny.

(b) On Procedural Part

(i) On Planning process at the appropriate level

Planning process is as important as the Plan itself. As a matter of fact, quality of the plan depends on its planning process. The importance of the planning process can be understood from the fact that the Constitution of India itself provided forum of Gram Sabha in the rural areas and Ward Sabha for the municipalities for consultations and sensoring public perception on planning items and its priorities. This apart, the Planning Commission, the State Government and the DPC usually issued guidelines for the planning process. It would be relevant to see whether the decentralised plans have been prepared on following broad guidelines and prior interaction and consultations with stake holders have taken place at the local level.

(ii) Consolidation process of preparation of draft district plan by the DPC

The DPC has to follow a step by step approach for consolidation of plans received from the Panchayats and the Municipalities so as to make the consolidation business meaningful from the planning angle. In doing so, it has to make use of meaningful tool for facilitating such consolidation. The transparent process made use of for such consolidation may also examined by the State.

Observations/comments of the State Planning Board or the State Government

The time –line is very important for any plan related job. The comments of the State Planning Board or the State Government have important bearing on follow-up actions to be taken within the financial year along with host of items incidental thereto. Therefore, it is of utmost importance that observations/comments on draft district plan are made known early to the DPC to enable to share the same with the levels of Panchayats and Municipalities for appropriate follow-up. Incidentally it may be relevant to mention that in view of pressing timelines and the statutory limitation, it may not always be possible to follow the same procedure afresh for resubmission of proposals as the related local body has to accord approval of the annual plan and secure budgetary sanction within statutory time limit. It would serve the purpose of compliance if the related local body effects the observations of the State Planning Board or the State Government at the time of its approval of Annual plan before budgetary sanction and communicate the same to the DPC. A copy of the Annual plan so approved and budgeted by the related local body may thereafter be sent to the DPC for record.

9

Implementation of Decentralised Plans

Implementation is the final destination for any scheme. By such implementation the inherent objectives of a scheme are actualised. The actualisation of objectives also helps to achieve the outcome of the scheme. Actualisation or implementation process is very challenging as it is linked with procedures, capacity building, timelines, funding, accounting, monitoring, etc.

In a Government system, there are laid down standard procedures before commencement of actual work of any scheme. It relates to preparation of scheme (Project Report for a very big scheme), its vetting at the appropriate level, and environmental clearance from the designated authority etc which in turn consume a sizable portion of prime time. The Expression of Interest, Tender, Quotations, Work order, etc are other areas that also take away a big chunk of work time for some big schemes. Time slippage and cost escalation restarts the whole process and affects original schedule of completion of works. Rainy season and weather factors also affect schedule of works. Besides, performances of some tasks are linked with quality, enhancement of capacity building and unless this part of requisites is addressed earlier it will encroach upon schedule of time lines. Another factor that delays the implementation proceedings is the absence of a check list to monitor for sequential actions.

The upshot of the discussion is that macro-image of the role of government sector as implementation agency is not very encouraging. The identified factors responsible for delay are not seriously addressed and the recurrence of similar maladies goes on. It is always a story of carried forward and a journey with continuing schemes of previous years. Further, the culture of release of considerable funds at the fag end of the financial year is not at all inspiring and implementation friendly; it leads to improper use of funds resulting in compromise on quality. The 'March syndrome' is the single biggest factor for poor quality of implementation of works.

Implementation issues relating to Decentralised Plans are also seldom addressed. Though there are common issues in implementation areas in between the government and local bodies, those are also different in many ways for decentralised plans. The presence of watchful stakeholders nearby and the compulsion to complete the sanctioned schemes in a time format are factors that directly and immediately impact the brand image of efficiency of the local bodies. The statutory requirement to present annual performance status in the constituency of the local body is another pressing contributory factor that works to complete schemes in time. Further, the local bodies usually take up relatively small schemes and make it easier to implement them early. The volume of completed schemes in a plan year is, therefore, likely to be several times higher than the completion status of government sector schemes. However, the number and timely completion of schemes by itself is not good enough; ensurance of the quality of completed schemes is the most important consideration and in this aspect the macro image of the local bodies is not that bright. Depending on the nature of scheme, the quality care requirement would also be varied and different. It would be of great help if standard quality care guidance by means of check list is designed and kept ready for its appropriate use at the stage of implementation and monitoring of schemes. Needless to mention, the local body would require to keep the stakeholders informed about the details of the scheme before commencement of the work and stakeholders' impression of the scheme after it is so completed as a part of social audit. In other words, a system of scheme-specific detailed plan of action is required to ensure core intention of a scheme and its timely completion.

There are other issues associated with implementation at this level. These are connected with compliance of norms for human development. Each unit of the local body is supposed to serve both as a service provider as well as an institutional auditor from human development angle. As a service provider, it has to take care to inclusive consideration by removing hurdles to access, enlarging choice, enhancing capabilities and ensuring participation. Based on human development deficit and having regard to the devolved institutional responsibility, it is required to address each of the components of human development at the time of implementation of schemes. As an institutional auditor, it has to examine whether the design of delivery of services for the intended beneficiaries has been appropriate for required outreach for the un-served and underserved areas, its envisioned outcome, its actual achievement and the possible areas for revisiting and course correction.

A corollary requirement in this area of implementation is publication of Annual Report or Annual Performance Report. It need not turn out to be a report of mere statements of release of funds and expenditure but must include the status of physical achievements in terms of its measurable units to indicate its real output and its linkage with outcome process. Each of the local bodies needs to publish and share it with stakeholders on a regular basis.

10

Monitoring of Decentralised Plans

Monitoring is defined as a process of measuring, recording, collecting, processing and communicating information to assist project management in decision making. Monitoring is a functioning tool to understand the flow character of a scheme right from the time of its commencement. It generates not only flow of data but deciphers also its inner meaning of the process behaviour signalling thereby the irritating points that need to be resolved. In that mould, it acts as supervising the functioning process to a particular work plan at a given point of time.

For productive monitoring four critical aspects need to be addressed:

(i) What is to be Monitored

Monitoring items should be pointed, relevant and critical. Such items include physical and financial progress. The items also include time dimension of completion of any scheme. Design of the monitoring format has to be structured accordingly. Further, the items for monitoring and items for monitoring meeting are different. Persistently surfacing problems need only to be the agenda item up for appropriate resolution in a monitoring meeting.

In the context of the decentralised local bodies, the broad subjects for monitoring items may be the schemes on devolved subjects and/or assigned subjects. It may also take up special monitoring on group of schemes relating to human development and the like.

(ii) Who is to Monitor

The primary responsibility of monitoring lies with the implementation authority. In the case of decentralised local bodies, it rests with the related local body. The Gram Panchayat will monitor implementation of its own schemes and so by others. There is no scope of monitoring a local body by another tier. However, the DPC, as the apex Constitutional planning body in the district may take up monitoring in respect of all schemes or for schemes falling under any selective subject (e.g. drinking water, road linkage, waste disposal, etc.) as it deems proper. Another important point in this regard is that monitoring team members must be well conversant with the schemes under monitoring review including its objects, other details and timelines of completion, etc. The domain knowledge of team members only ensures meaningful interactions.

(iii) How to Monitor them

The implementing unit needs to fill in designed monitoring format as per time design and submit to its local body. Normally, the descriptive version should not be encouraged for the sake of easier comprehension and its consolidation. Based on analysis of monitoring data, a status position is needed to be worked out. The monitoring status, with observations if any, may then be communicated to all concerned for appropriate action. In case of necessity, it could be followed up by field inspection as well. A monitoring meeting may also be convened to sort out implementation issues for the desired way forward.

(iv) Monitoring of Action taken Report

Monitoring is for ensuring right course of programme implementation and, therefore, it is not a one time affair. It is a continuous process till the scheme is completed. The prescriptions for correction based on a monitoring report, say MR- 1, need to be comprehensively addressed before submitting monitoring report, say MR- 2. Mere communication of findings without follow-up compliance report would make the entire exercise redundant. ATR is in fact the essence of monitoring.

Monitoring *per se* is not an end in itself. It is a means to ensure proper implementation of scheme by acting as an indivisible supervisor during the process of implementation. Moreover, it is not enough that monitoring technique should be applied alone: it is also required to be buttressed by the other technique known as concurrent evaluation. In fact, monitoring and concurrent evaluation are two activities which go hand in hand. Adequate monitoring is a basic requisite for undertaking concurrent evaluation and it is impossible to evaluate a scheme unless it has been adequately monitored over time.

11

Coordination and Convergence in the Decentralised Platform

Coordination and Convergence of schemes have important functional roles for local bodies' cumulative efforts to register productive governance. Coordination is the act of working together for a goal or effect. Coordination is also a platform in which mutual gains are reaped if participants make mutually consistent decisions. All irritating roadblocks standing in the path of programme implementation area are taken up in the coordination meet for resolution.

From operational angle, the most important layer of coordination is those connected with actual execution of schemes or those connected with its immediate supervision. The administrative culture obtaining in the field, however, call for the crucial role of a third party facilitator with an independent image to preside over such coordination interactions and the institution of the District Magistrate has emerged as an acceptable coordination maker in most of the districts in the country. As a result, the District Magistrate assumes crucial role in coordination and presides over a number of coordination meetings designed for bilateral partners or for plural number of stake holders like district development or subject specific coordination like irrigation, disaster management, sports, law and order, and the like. The essence of this coordination committee meeting is to remove hurdles and reordering operational linkages and connectivity between one programme and the other for better output. An illustration may be given. The target for Boro paddy cultivable area of the Agriculture department depends to a great extent on assured and timely release of specified quantum of water by the Irrigation department. Unless the time sequence and the requisite quantum of water are made available, the target on Boro cultivation will fail. The coordination efforts would make the action process easier.

Co-ordination Architecture

The historical role played by the institution of the District Magistrate in the planning and development area of coordination is now being taken up in the forum of the District Planning Committee (DPC) subsequent to the emergence of the DPC as the focal point on development and the Chairperson of DPC along with the District Magistrate conduct such coordination meeting. It covers all plan related coordination issues between the Panchayats and the Municipalities. It also addresses coordination issues among various other development partners working in those areas. The architecture of coordination partners may be described as follows:

(a) Coordination among three tiers of Panchayats

(b) Coordination among the tiers of Panchayats and the Municipalities

(c) Coordination among the Municipalities

(d) Coordination among the line departments in the district and the tiers of Panchayats and the Municipalities

(e) Coordination among the Parastatal bodies and the tiers of Panchayats and the Municipalities

(f) Coordination among the NGOs and the tiers of Panchayats and the Municipalities

(g) Coordination among the Financial Institutions and the tiers of Panchayats and the Municipalities

Functional Universe of Coordination

Based on the constitutional empowerment, the functional universe of coordination in the decentralized forum may fall on areas as mentioned below:

(i) Coordination on Linkage among Programmes devolved on to the local bodies for better output

Based on the 11th Schedule and the principle of subsidiarity, the functional devolution among the Village Panchayat, Block Panchayat and Zilla Panchayat may be on very inter-connected programme e.g. the road network may be interconnected with Village Panchayats, Block Panchayats and Zilla Panchayats and that coordination among them is required both in respect of upgradation, improvement and maintenance to have desired output from the entire road network within a time format. Similarly, such coordination may be constantly needed on agriculture related functional items like distribution of minikits, extension education, distribution of surface irrigation and ground water, timing of power supply, storage of food grains, etc. In other words, intra Panchayat programme issues could be key coordination items.

(ii) Coordination on Environmental Initiatives

Environment management is extremely difficult and requires backward and forward support of development partners. Inter-linkages and connectivity of complementary, supportive and linked programmes need periodical coordination meet to ensure that all components of environmental initiatives are addressed in a linked and proper manner for wholesome impact.

(iii) *Coordination on Spatial Issues Including Water Bodies, Sanitation and Waste Disposal*

Ever increasing density of population is usually reflected in encroachment on water bodies, problems in sanitary and drainage problems and more particularly on waste disposal front and generate tension among the rural and urban local bodies.This is a very crucial area of coordination for the DPC for maintaining environmental and developmental balance in the district.

The big area of coordination is, however, for settling spatial and programme related issues among the Gram Panchayats, Block Panchayats, Zilla Panchayat and the Municipalities. Frictional noises, jurisdictional issue, negative fall-out of given programme, emerging complementary role of another local body etc., are items that need to be comprehensively resolved in specially convened coordination meeting in a spirit of accommodation.

The high valued platform of coordination meeting requires to be structured with due care and caution. Only coordinating functionaries at the appropriate level of the related institutions/ departments need to be invited for interactions- for being in a position to participate in the decision taking exercises with authority and also empowered to follow them up. The token presence by a proxy representative does serve only notional value. Such a meeting needs to be preceded by situational analysis of implementation areas, the sources of causal factors of hurdles that have surfaced and possible role of stake holding institutions/departments for removal or redressal of hurdles. Thus, an in-depth home work on what and how aspect is a necessary condition for productive coordination. Otherwise, it would turn out to be an exercise of a ritual and nothing positive would come out of it. The sufficient condition for productive coordination is to publish an ATR (Action Taken Report) on decisions earlier taken in a previous coordination meeting.

Convergence

Another area linked with coordination is Convergence. As a matter of fact, coordination spirit is a necessary condition for convergence.Convergence indeed is a bigger functional concept implicit in which exists a framework of programme connectivity, a shared goal and focused output at a possible incremental scale. The presence of a lead scheme is the essential pre-requisite. The schemes for convergent partnership could be collaborative, supportive, connected, linked, associated or additive. The bonding of convergence might be triggered by synergy; it might as well be driven by forces of investment or on spatial planning consideration. Such partnership may take the form of dovetailing; it may as well take the form of tie-up accommodation or it may converge under one window. The convergent junction has to be a shared work-out node based on activity mapping and also properly sequenced. However, the architecture of convergence in the decentralised set-up may be shown separately as below:

(a) Convergence of Schemes among Three Tiers of Panchayats

Under Article 243G, the concerned State Government is required to devolve functional items of the Eleventh Schedule of the Constitution of India on to levels of Panchayats separately for each tier of the Panchayat. The mandate for Panchayat tier-wise devolution is very relevant for the functional identity of an organisation and to the growth of the local self government. However, in a limited number of States only devolution has taken place giving rise to possibilities of convergence within the schemes of the particular tier of the Panchayats, with schemes of other tiers of the Panchayats and finally with schemes of the line departments of the government. The moot point in facilitating convergence is that such schemes would have to be compatible and its location would be in a continuous geographical situation.

Besides, tiers of Panchayats, bordering a municipality often face real challenge of local development requiring co-ordinated, linked and convergent schemes for continuum development. These could be in the area of road network, drainage, garbage disposal, drinking water and the like. Even the MLALD schemes could be fitted in local areas under convergent mode. Rural-Urban convergence is thus emerging as a big area of convergence in local area development to maximise limited resources for optimal output.

Further, a large number of NGOs and Self-help groups of various descriptions perform development functions as parallel agencies, unconnected, very often, with any scheme either of a particular tier of Panchayat or of a department in the government. The possible scope for scheme specific convergence with such schemes of such agencies needs also to be explored, where ever feasible.

Finally, the big area of convergence lies with schemes of a particular tier of Panchayat with the schemes of the government-both central and the state in the given geographical area. The scope and nature of convergence have to be worked out cautiously having regard to competence level of the tier of Panchayat, the compatible nature of such short-listed schemes, the time format of execution, etc.

(b) Convergence among the Schemes of the Municipality

The Municipalities are required to perform 18 functions as enshrined in the 12th Schedule after its empowerment by the state government. Earlier municipalities used to perform mostly regulatory and non-plan related nature of works. The new constitutional mandate made them equal partners in plan related works as well and the municipalities are now the new hub of urban development initiatives. Consequently within such municipal works, the scope for convergence among schemes has emerged. Further, a good number of municipalities exist side by side in geographical locations requiring interconnectivity and programme linkage among themselves on a number of items for wider outreach and also for broadening the local regional development. The scope for programme convergence among such municipalities has also emerged in this area. Besides, the big state sector or district sector schemes of the line departments of the government very often fall in the urban areas requiring adjustments, coordination and possible convergence with schemes of municipalities, wherever feasible.

(c) Convergence of Schemes of Prastatal bodies and the Panchayats / Municipalities

Prastatal bodies continue to exist in different States by virtue of state legislations even after the 73rd and the 74th Amendments of the Constitution. Such bodies usually function as development agencies; in some cases, it also functions as land use planning agency. The existence of such parallel agencies on the functional domain area of the Panchayats/ Municipalities is a grey area of decentralised development administration .It also stands as positive irritant in functional devolution. The Second Administrative Reforms Commission also deliberated on the issue and recommended to revisit the area by the concerned government and take appropriate action to reorganise such prastatals. Pending reforms in this area, it would be only desirable that schemes taken up by Parastatals and the Panchayats at the appropriate level or the Municipalities need to avoid duplication of efforts. Effective co-ordination has to be put in place for optimizing return of investment. The scope for convergence on scheme specific areas needs to be worked out by mutual dialogue and interaction.

(d) Convergence among Programmes of the NGOs with others

The Civil societies and NGOs have considerably spread in the state driven by commitment and agenda for development. The Government of India has also drawn up National Policy on voluntary Sector specifying areas where NGOs have functional role and space. The Planning Commission and the UN system look forward to the positive role of such NGOs and nourish them with patronage and funds. In large number of cases such NGOs work as parallel agencies without mainstreaming their activities with the nodal schemes of the government or the local bodies. The need for working together in a particular development- function area either with the tiers of the

Panchayat or the Municipalities for greater outreach and better outcome, as a shared responsibility, can hardly be over emphasised. This is a critical area for coordination and convergence.

(e) Convergence with Other Agencies

Private institution and Private Trusts very often take up a number of schemes specially in the social sector with philanthropic as well as commercial motives. Considering the nature of organisation and its cultural behaviour it is probable, in selective cases, to have functioning linkage and in some exceptional cases scheme related convergence too, either with other private players or with schemes of the tiers of the Panchayat or the Municipalities.

Financial institutions have varying portfolio of schemes from one institution to another. Further under financial inclusion, they stretch out in hitherto un-chartered locations and hitherto uncovered clients. Incidentally under the same inclusive approach the line departments of the government, the tiers of the Panchayat or the Municipalities take up a number of schemes which may also have credit component or credit linkage. This is an under-served territory for field level coordination and convergence.

Incidentally it may be worthwhile to mention that Convergence has no universal applicability, nor is it open to convergent negotiations. As a matter of fact, all schemes are not convergent friendly and convergent dependent at all and would do justice if compatible convergent friendly schemes are worked out for guidance for field level functionaries to insulate against convergent craze.

Short-listing of convergent friendly schemes is also important from other considerations. The limitation of human angle, audit angle and programme specific target angle has also to be taken into consideration in such convergence initiatives. A required level of knowledge and skill is *sin qua non* for true convergence.

Role of the District Planning Committee as Convergent maker

The District Planning Committee has come into being in almost all the states of India as a compliance of the mandatory provision of Article 243ZD. The Constitution provides that DPC is to consolidate plans prepared by the Panchayats and the Municipalities. The Panchayats and the Municipalities are also implementing bodies in respect of their schemes.

Convergence is an operational process and functionally relevant at the execution level. The operational test of convergence is in the field where schemes are taken up for implementation. Such convergence may arise with schemes falling under state sector, district sector or with both of them. Within district sector schemes, it may be limited to departmental schemes of the state government, within schemes of the tiers of the Panchayat or at the municipality or with any programme-partner or combination of partners having compatible schemes for working on convergence. Such compatible schemes could be on areas of livelihood, elementary education, heath care, nutrition care, gender empowerment, tribal welfare and the like.

Now, consolidation is the primary function of the DPC which is more of aggregating developmental function, heads of development wise, and less of a planning function. In regard to linkage between consolidations with convergence, it may be stated that the process of consolidation of plans and the process of convergence are quite different. While consolidation is a process of aggregation of inputs, convergence is a process to ensure incremental output. Convergence as such does not exist as an element in the exercise of consolidation and that mere consolidation does not lead to any convergence at all.

The role of local body in the area of convergence may be seen from a different perspective. During the envisioning and stock taking stage of planning the local body would be in a position to understand where synergy is called for, where coordinated efforts between work-agencies would ensure targeted output or where convergence in between schemes is required to optimise outcome of investment. From that stage on, the local body may work on possible convergence, interact with convergent partner and design checklist for actions. Once such an exercise is made, the preliminary convergence action plan would be ready. It will then enable the particular Panchayat to monitor step by step the process of implementation through the related work agencies. The process could also be the same for the municipalities as well. The diversity of local conditions might need minor adjustments and different kind of adaptations.

The proximity to the work areas is thus a necessary requirement for convergence monitoring. The existence of a unit of local body in the work area is a natural advantage to remain updated with stages of implementation on the convergent pathway. This kind of hand-holding responsibility on convergence, can be performed by the local body in place only. The DPC can at best play a secondary role on convergent monitoring to inform how the primary levels are taking care of their roles and the need to revisit some options.

There is, however, a different but distinct role of the DPC in matters relating to convergence. The on-field frictional noises arising out of political character of the competing local bodies, jurisdictional issues, rural-urban issues or otherwise, may require deft handling for its resolution by a superior authority. The forum of the DPC is best suited to play the role as convergent ombudsmen.

Acronyms

AID	Acquired Immuno Deficiency Syndrome
APL	Above the Poverty Line
ATR	Action Taken Report
AWP	Annual Works Programme
BP	Block Panchayat
BPL	Below the Poverty Line
BRGF	Backward Region Grant Fund
CAD&WM	Command Area Development and Water Management
DHDR	District Human Development Report
DLBC	District Level Bankers Committee
DPC	District Planning Committee
DRDA	District Rural Development Agency
DPR	Detailed Project Report
EWG	Economically Weaker Group
FAO	Food and Agricultural Organisation
GOI	Government of India
GP	Gram Panchayat
GPS	Geographical Position System
GS	Gram Sabha
IAY	Indira Awas Yojana
ICDS	Integrated Child Development Services
ICAR	Indian Council of Agricultural Research
ILO	International Labour Organisation
IMR	Infant Mortality Rate/Ratio

IRDP	Integrated Rural Development Programme
IWMP	Integrated Watershed Management Programme
JFMC	Joint Forest Management Committee
JNNURM	Jawaharlal Nehru National Urban Renewal Mission
JSY	Janani Suraksha Yojana
KVK	Krishi Vikas Kendra
KVS	Krishi Vikas Sevak
MDG	Millennium Development Goals
MGNRESS	Mahatma Gandhi National Rural Employment Service Scheme
MNP	Minimum Needs Programme
MoA	Ministry of Agriculture
MoRD	Ministry of Rural Development
MoWR	Ministry of Water Resources
MPC	Metropolitan Planning Committee
MPLAD	Member of Parliament's Local Area Development
NAP	National Afforestation Programme
NGO	Non Governmental Organisation
NRDMS	Natural Resources Data Base Management System
NREGA	National Rural Employment Guarantee Act
NREGS	National Rural Employment Guarantee Scheme
NRHM	National Rural Health Mission
NWDPRA	National Watershed Development Project in Rain fed Areas
PIA	Project Implementation Authority
PMGSY	Prime Miniter's Gram Sadak Yojana
PWD	Public Works Department
RKVY	Rastriya Krishi Vikas Yojana
RSVY	Rastriya Sam Vikas Yojana
SC/ST	Scheduled Caste/Scheduled Tribe
SCSP	Scheduled Caste Sub Plan
SFC	State Finance Commission
SHG	Self Help Groups
SGSY	Swarna Jayanti Grameen Swarogar Yojana

SLSC	State Level Selection Committee
SSA	Sarva Shiksha Abhiyan
TFR	Total Fertility Rate
TSC	Total Sanitation Campaign
TSP	Tribal Sub Plan
UIDSST	Urban Infrastructure Development Scheme in Satellite Town
UIDSSMT	Urban Infrastructure Development Scheme for Small and Medium Town.
UNAIDS	United Nations Programme on AIDS
UNDAF	United Nations Development Assistance Framework
UNICEF	United Nations International Children's Emergency Fund
UNEP	United Nations Environment Programme
UNFPA	United Nations Fund for Population Assistance
UNO	United Nations Organisation
WHO	World Health Organisation
ZP	Zilla Panchayat

Appendices - 1

Extracts from the Constitution of India

PART IX

THE PANCHAYATS

243. In this Part, unless the context otherwise requires,—

(*a*) "district" means a district in a State;

(*b*) "Gram Sabha" means a body consisting of persons registered in the electoral rolls relating to a village comprised within the area of Panchayat at the village level;

(*c*) "intermediate level" means a level between the village and district levels specified by the Governor of a State by public notification to be the intermediate level for the purposes of this Part;

(*d*) "Panchayat" means an institution (by whatever name called) of self-government constituted under Article 243B, for the rural areas;

(*e*) "Panchayat area" means the territorial area of a Panchayat;

243B. (1) There shall be constituted in every State, Panchayats at the village, intermediate and district levels in accordance with the provisions of this Part.

(2) Notwithstanding anything in clause (1), Panchayats at the intermediate level may not be constituted in a State having a population not exceeding twenty lakhs.

1[PART IXA

THE MUNICIPALITIES

243P. In this Part, unless the context otherwise requires,—

(*a*) "Committee" means a Committee constituted under Article 243S;

(*b*) "district" means a district in a State;

(*c*) "Metropolitan area" means an area having a population of ten lakhs or more, comprised in one or more districts and consisting of two or more Municipalities or Panchayats or other contiguous areas, specified by the Governor by public notification to be a Metropolitan area for the purposes of this Part;

(*d*) "Municipal area" means the territorial area of a Municipality as is notified by the Governor;

(*e*) "Municipality" means an institution of self government constituted under Article 243Q;

243Q. (1) There shall be constituted in every State,—

(*a*) a Nagar Panchayat (by whatever name called) for a transitional area, that is to say, an area in transition from a rural area to an urban area;

(*b*) a Municipal Council for a smaller urban area; and

(*c*) a Municipal Corporation for a larger urban area, in accordance with the provisions of this Part:

Provided that a Municipality under this clause may not be constituted in such urban area or part thereof as the Governor may, having regard to the size of the area and the municipal services being provided or proposed to be provided by an industrial establishment in that area and such other factors as he may deem fit, by public notification, specify to be an industrial township.

(2) In this Article, "a transitional area", "a smaller urban area" or "a larger urban area" means such area as the Governor may, having regard to the population of the area, the density of the population therein, the revenue generated for local administration, the percentage of

employment in non-agricultural activities, the economic importance or such other factors as he may deem fit, specify by public notification for the purposes of this Part.

Powers, authority and responsibilities of Panchayats.

243G. Subject to the provisions of this Constitution, the Legislature of a State may, by law, endow the Panchayats with such powers and authority as may be necessary to enable them to function as institutions of self-government and such law may contain provisions for the devolution of powers and responsibilities upon Panchayats at the appropriate level, subject to such conditions as may be specified therein, with respect to—

(*a*) the preparation of plans for economic development and social justice;

(*b*) the implementation of schemes for economic development and social justice as may be entrusted to them including those in relation to the matters listed in the Eleventh Schedule.

Powers, authority and responsibilities of Municipalities, etc.

243W. Subject to the provisions of this Constitution, the Legislature of a State may, by law, endow—

(*a*) the Municipalities with such powers and authority as may be necessary to enable them to function as institutions of self-government and such law may contain provisions for the devolution of powers and responsibilities upon Municipalities, subject to such conditions as may be specified therein with respect to—

  (*i*) the preparation of plans for economic development and social justice;

  (*ii*) the performance of functions and the implementation of schemes as may be entrusted to them including those in relation to the matters listed in the Twelfth Schedule;

(*b*) the Committees with such powers and authority as may be necessary to enable them to carry out the responsibilities conferred upon them including those in relation to the matters listed in the Twelfth Schedule. Committee for district planning.

243ZD. (1) There shall be constituted in every State at the district level a District Planning Committee to consolidate the plans prepared by the Panchayats and the Municipalities in the district and to prepare a draft development plan for the district as a whole.

(2) The Legislature of a State may, by law, make provision with respect to—

(*a*) the composition of the District Planning Committees;

(*b*) the manner in which the seats in such Committees shall be filled:

Provided that not less than four-fifths of the total number of members of such Committee shall be elected by, and from amongst, the elected members of the Panchayat at the district level and of the Municipalities in the district in proportion to the ratio between the population of the rural areas and of the urban areas in the district;

(*c*) the functions relating to district planning which may be assigned to such Committees;

(*d*) the manner in which the Chairpersons of such Committees shall be chosen.

(3) Every District Planning Committee shall, in preparing the draft development plan,—

(*a*) have regard to—

(*i*) matters of common interest between the Panchayats and the Municipalities including spatial planning, sharing of water and other physical and natural resources, the integrated development of infrastructure and environmental conservation;

(*ii*) the extent and type of available resources whether financial or otherwise;

(*b*) consult such institutions and organisations as the Governor may, by order, specify.

(4) The Chairperson of every District Planning Committee shall forward the development plan, as recommended by such Committee, to the Government of the State.

Appendix - 1.1

SEVENTH SCHEDULE

(Article 246)

List I—Union List

1. Defence of India and every part thereof including preparation for defence and all such acts as may be conducive in times of war to its prosecution and after its termination to effective demobilisation.
2. Naval, military and air forces; any other armed forces of the Union.1[2A. Deployment of any armed force of the Union or any other force subject to the control of the Union or any contingent or unit thereof in any State in aid of the civil power; powers, jurisdiction, privileges and liabilities of the members of such forces while on such deployment.]
3. Delimitation of cantonment areas, local self-government in such areas, the constitution and powers within such areas of cantonment authorities and the regulation of house accommodation (including the control of rents) in such areas.
4. Naval, military and air force works.
5. Arms, firearms, ammunition and explosives.
6. Atomic energy and mineral resources necessary for its production.

7. Industries declared by Parliament by law to be necessary for the purpose of defence or for the prosecution of war.
8. Central Bureau of Intelligence and Investigation.
9. Preventive detention for reasons connected with Defence, Foreign Affairs, or the security of India; persons subjected to such detention.
10. Foreign affairs; all matters which bring the Union into relation with any foreign country.
11. Diplomatic, consular and trade representation.
12. United Nations Organisation.
13. Participation in international conferences, associations and other bodies and implementing of decisions made thereat.
14. Entering into treaties and agreements with foreign countries and implementing of treaties, agreements and conventions with foreign countries.
15. War and peace.
16. Foreign jurisdiction.
17. Citizenship, naturalisation and aliens.
18. Extradition.
19. Admission into, and emigration and expulsion from, India; passports and visas.
20. Pilgrimages to places outside India.
21. Piracies and crimes committed on the high seas or in the air; offences against the law of nations committed on land or the high seas or in the air.
22. Railways.
23. Highways declared by or under law made by Parliament to be national highways.
24. Shipping and navigation on inland waterways, declared by Parliament by law to be national waterways, as regards mechanically propelled vessels; the rule of the road on such waterways.
25. Maritime shipping and navigation, including shipping and navigation on tidal waters; provision of education and training for the mercantile marine and regulation of such

education and training provided by States and other agencies.

26. Lighthouses, including lightships, beacons and other provision for the safety of shipping and aircraft.
27. Ports declared by or under law made by Parliament or existing law to be major ports, including their delimitation, and the constitution and powers of port authorities therein.
28. Port quarantine, including hospitals connected therewith; seamen's and marine hospitals.
29. Airways; aircraft and air navigation; provision of aerodromes; regulation and organisation of air traffic and of aerodromes; provision for aeronautical education and training and regulation of such education and training provided by States and other agencies.
30. Carriage of passengers and goods by railway, sea or air, or by national waterways in mechanically propelled vessels.
31. Posts and telegraphs; telephones, wireless, broadcasting and other like forms of communication.
32. Property of the Union and the revenue therefrom, but as regards property situated in a State 1*** subject to legislation by the State, save in so far as Parliament by law otherwise provides.
34. Courts of wards for the estates of Rulers of Indian States.
35. Public debt of the Union.
36. Currency, coinage and legal tender; foreign exchange.
37. Foreign loans.
38. Reserve Bank of India.
39. Post Office Savings Bank.
40. Lotteries organised by the Government of India or the Government of a State.
41. Trade and commerce with foreign countries; import and export across customs frontiers; definition of customs frontiers.
42. Inter-State trade and commerce.

43. Incorporation, regulation and winding up of trading corporations, including banking, insurance and financial corporations, but not including co-operative societies.
44. Incorporation, regulation and winding up of corporations, whether trading or not, with objects not confined to one State, but not including universities.
45. Banking.
46. Bills of exchange, cheques, promissory notes and other like instruments.
47. Insurance.
48. Stock exchanges and futures markets.
49. Patents, inventions and designs; copyright; trade-marks and merchandise marks.
50. Establishment of standards of weight and measure.
51. Establishment of standards of quality for goods to be exported out of India or transported from one State to another.
52. Industries, the control of which by the Union is declared by Parliament by law to be expedient in the public interest.
53. Regulation and development of oilfields and mineral oil resources; petroleum and petroleum products; other liquids and substances declared by Parliament by law to be dangerously inflammable.
54. Regulation of mines and mineral development to the extent to which such regulation and development under the control of the Union is declared by Parliament by law to be expedient in the public interest.
55. Regulation of labour and safety in mines and oilfields.
56. Regulation and development of inter-State rivers and river valleys to the extent to which such regulation and development under the control of the Union is declared by Parliament by law to be expedient in the public interest.
57. Fishing and fisheries beyond territorial waters.
58. Manufacture, supply and distribution of salt by Union agencies; regulation and control of manufacture, supply and distribution of salt by other agencies.

59. Cultivation, manufacture, and sale for export, of opium.
60. Sanctioning of cinematograph films for exhibition.
61. Industrial disputes concerning Union employees.
62. The institutions known at the commencement of this Constitution as the National Library, the Indian Museum, the Imperial War Museum, the Victoria Memorial and the Indian War Memorial, and any other like institution financed by the Government of India wholly or in part and declared by Parliament by law to be an institution of national importance.
63. The institutions known at the commencement of this Constitution as the Benares Hindu University, the Aligarh Muslim University and the 1[Delhi University; the University established in pursuance of Article 371E;] any other institution declared by Parliament by law to be an institution of national importance.
64. Institutions for scientific or technical education financed by the Government of India wholly or in part and declared by Parliament by law to be institutions of national importance.
65. Union agencies and institutions for—
    (a) professional, vocational or technical training, including the training of police officers; or
    (b) the promotion of special studies or research; or
    (c) scientific or technical assistance in the investigation or detection of crime.
66. Co-ordination and determination of standards in institutions for higher education or research and scientific and technical institutions.
67. Ancient and historical monuments and records, and archaeological sites and remains, 1[declared by or under law made by Parliament] to be of national importance.
68. The Survey of India, the Geological, Botanical, Zoological and Anthropological Surveys of India; Meteorological organisations.
69. Census.

70. Union Public Service; All-India Services; Union Public Service Commission.
71. Union pensions, that is to say, pensions payable by the Government of India or out of the Consolidated Fund of India.
72. Elections to Parliament, to the Legislatures of States and to the offices of President and Vice-President; the Election Commission.
73. Salaries and allowances of members of Parliament, the Chairman and Deputy Chairman of the Council of States and the Speaker and Deputy Speaker of the House of the People.
74. Powers, privileges and immunities of each House of Parliament and of the members and the Committees of each House; enforcement of attendance of persons for giving evidence or producing documents before committees of Parliament or commissions appointed by Parliament.
75. Emoluments, allowances, privileges, and rights in respect of leave of absence, of the President and Governors; salaries and allowances of the Ministers for the Union; the salaries, allowances, and rights in respect of leave of absence and other conditions of service of the Comptroller and Auditor-General.
76. Audit of the accounts of the Union and of the States.
77. Constitution, organisation, jurisdiction and powers of the Supreme Court (including contempt of such Court), and the fees taken therein; persons entitled to practise before the Supreme Court.
78. Constitution and organisation 1[(including vacations)] of the High Courts except provisions as to officers and servants of High Courts; persons entitled to practise before the High Courts.
79. Extension of the jurisdiction of a High Court to, and exclusion of the jurisdiction of a High Court from, any Union territory.]

80. Extension of the powers and jurisdiction of members of a police force belonging to any State to any area outside that State, but not so as to enable the police of one State to exercise powers and jurisdiction in any area outside that State without the consent of the Government of the State in which such area is situated; extension of the powers and jurisdiction of members of a police force belonging to any State to railway areas outside that State.
81. Inter-State migration; inter-State quarantine.
82. Taxes on income other than agricultural income.
83. Duties of customs including export duties.
84. Duties of excise on tobacco and other goods manufactured or produced in India except—
    (*a*) alcoholic liquors for human consumption;
    (*b*) opium, Indian hemp and other narcotic drugs and narcotics, but including medicinal and toilet preparations containing alcohol or any substance included in sub-paragraph (*b*) of this entry.
85. Corporation tax.
86. Taxes on the capital value of the assets, exclusive of agricultural land, of individuals and companies; taxes on the capital of companies.
87. Estate duty in respect of property other than agricultural land.
88. Duties in respect of succession to property other than agricultural land.
89. Terminal taxes on goods or passengers, carried by railway, sea or air; taxes on railway fares and freights.
90. Taxes other than stamp duties on transactions in stock exchanges and futures markets.
91. Rates of stamp duty in respect of bills of exchange, cheques, promissory notes, bills of lading, letters of credit, policies of insurance, transfer of shares, debentures, proxies and receipts.
92. Taxes on the sale or purchase of newspapers and on advertisements published therein.

1[92A. Taxes on the sale or purchase of goods other than newspapers, where such sale or purchase takes place in the course of inter-State trade or commerce.]

2[92B. Taxes on the consignments of goods (whether the consignment is to the person making it or to any other person), where such consignment takes place in the course of inter-State trade or commerce.]

*[92C. Taxes on services.]

93. Offences against laws with respect to any of the matters in this List.

94. Inquiries, surveys and statistics for the purpose of any of the matters in this List.

95. Jurisdiction and powers of all courts, except the Supreme Court, with respect to any of the matters in this List; admiralty jurisdiction.

96. Fees in respect of any of the matters in this List, but not including fees taken in any court.

97. Any other matter not enumerated in List II or List III including any tax not mentioned in either of those Lists.

List II—State List

1. Public order (but not including 3[the use of any naval, military or air force or any other armed force of the Union or of any other force subject to the control of the Union or of any contingent or unit thereof] in aid of the civil power).

1[2. Police (including railway and village police) subject to the provisions of entry 2A of List I.]

3.2***Officers and servants of the High Court; procedure in rent and revenue courts; fees taken in all courts except the Supreme Court.

4. Prisons, reformatories, Borstal institutions and other institutions of a like nature, and persons detained therein; arrangements with other States for the use of prisons and other institutions.

5. Local government, that is to say, the constitution and powers of municipal corporations, improvement trusts, districts boards, mining settlement authorities and other local authorities for the purpose of local selfgovernment or village administration.
6. Public health and sanitation; hospitals and dispensaries.
7. Pilgrimages, other than pilgrimages to places outside India.
8. Intoxicating liquors, that is to say, the production, manufacture, possession, transport, purchase and sale of intoxicating liquors.
9. Relief of the disabled and unemployable.
10. Burials and burial grounds; cremations and cremation grounds.

* ****

12. Libraries, museums and other similar institutions controlled or financed by the State; ancient and historical monuments and records other than those 4[declared by or under law made by Parliament] to be of national importance.
13. Communications, that is to say, roads, bridges, ferries, and other means of communication not specified in List I; municipal tramways; ropeways; inland waterways and traffic thereon subject to the provisions of List I and List III with regard to such waterways; vehicles other than mechanically propelled vehicles.
14. Agriculture, including agricultural education and research, protection against pests and prevention of plant diseases.
15. Preservation, protection and improvement of stock and prevention of animal diseases; veterinary training and practice.
16. Pounds and the prevention of cattle trespass.
17. Water, that is to say, water supplies, irrigation and canals, drainage and embankments, water storage and water power subject to the provisions of entry 56 of List I.

18. Land, that is to say, rights in or over land, land tenures including the relation of landlord and tenant, and the collection of rents; transfer and alienation of agricultural land; land improvement and agricultural loans; colonization.

* * * * *

21. Fisheries.
22. Courts of wards subject to the provisions of entry 34 of List I; encumbered and attached estates.
23. Regulation of mines and mineral development subject to the provisions of List I with respect to regulation and development under the control of the Union.
24. Industries subject to the provisions of 2 [entries 7 and 52] of List I.
25. Gas and gas-works.
26. Trade and commerce within the State subject to the provisions of entry 33 of List III.
27. Production, supply and distribution of goods subject to the provisions of entry 33 of List III.
28. Markets and fairs.

* * * * *

30. Money-lending and money-lenders; relief of agricultural indebtedness.
31. Inns and inn-keepers.
32. Incorporation, regulation and winding up of corporations, other than those specified in List I, and universities; unincorporated trading, literary, scientific, religious and other societies and associations; co-operative societies.
33. Theatres and dramatic performances; cinemas subject to the provisions of entry 60 of List I; sports, entertainments and amusements.
34. Betting and gambling.
35. Works, lands and buildings vested in or in the possession of the State.

* * * * *

37. Elections to the Legislature of the State subject to the provisions of any law made by Parliament.

38. Salaries and allowances of members of the Legislature of the State, of the Speaker and Deputy Speaker of the Legislative Assembly and, if there is a Legislative Council, of the Chairman and Deputy Chairman thereof.
39. Powers, privileges and immunities of the Legislative Assembly and of the members and the committees thereof, and, if there is a Legislative Council, of that Council and of the members and the committees thereof; enforcement of attendance of persons for giving evidence or producing documents before committees of the Legislature of the State.
40. Salaries and allowances of Ministers for the State.
41. State public services; State Public Service Commission.
42. State pensions, that is to say, pensions payable by the State or out of the Consolidated Fund of the State.
43. Public debt of the State.
44. Treasure trove.
45. Land revenue, including the assessment and collection of revenue, the maintenance of land records, survey for revenue purposes and records of rights, and alienation of revenues.
46. Taxes on agricultural income.
47. Duties in respect of succession to agricultural land.
48. Estate duty in respect of agricultural land.
49. Taxes on lands and buildings.
50. Taxes on mineral rights subject to any limitations imposed by Parliament by law relating to mineral development.
51. Duties of excise on the following goods manufactured or produced in the State and countervailing duties at the same or lower rates on similar goods manufactured or produced elsewhere in India:—
    (*a*) alcoholic liquors for human consumption;
    (*b*) opium, Indian hemp and other narcotic drugs and narcotics; but not including medicinal and toilet preparations containing alcohol or any substance included in sub-paragraph (*b*) of this entry.

52. Taxes on the entry of goods into a local area for consumption, use orsale therein.
53. Taxes on the consumption or sale of electricity.
1[54. Taxes on the sale or purchase of goods other than newspapers, subject to the provisions of entry 92A of List I.
55. Taxes on advertisements other than advertisements published in the newspapers 2 [and advertisements broadcast by radio or television].
56. Taxes on goods and passengers carried by road or on inland waterways.
57. Taxes on vehicles, whether mechanically propelled or not, suitable for use on roads, including tramcars subject to the provisions of entry 35 of List III.
58. Taxes on animals and boats.
59. Tolls.
60. Taxes on professions, trades, callings and employments.
61. Capitation taxes.
62. Taxes on luxuries, including taxes on entertainments, amusements, betting and gambling.
63. Rates of stamp duty in respect of documents other than those specified in the provisions of List I with regard to rates of stamp duty.
64. Offences against laws with respect to any of the matters in this List.
65. Jurisdiction and powers of all courts, except the Supreme Court, with respect to any of the matters in this List.
66. Fees in respect of any of the matters in this List, but not including fees taken in any court.

List III—Concurrent List

1. Criminal law, including all matters included in the Indian Penal Code at the commencement of this Constitution but excluding offences against laws with respect to any of the matters specified in List I or List II and excluding the

use of naval, military or air forces or any other armed forces of the Union in aid of the civil power.

2. Criminal procedure, including all matters included in the Code of Criminal Procedure at the commencement of this Constitution.
3. Preventive detention for reasons connected with the security of a State, the maintenance of public order, or the maintenance of supplies and services essential to the community; persons subjected to such detention.
4. Removal from one State to another State of prisoners, accused persons and persons subjected to preventive detention for reasons specified in entry 3 of this List.
5. Marriage and divorce; infants and minors; adoption; wills, intestacy and succession; joint family and partition; all matters in respect of which parties in judicial proceedings were immediately before the commencement of this Constitution subject to their personal law.
6. Transfer of property other than agricultural land; registration of deeds and documents.
7. Contracts, including partnership, agency, contracts of carriage, and other special forms of contracts, but not including contracts relating to agricultural land.
8. Actionable wrongs.
9. Bankruptcy and insolvency.
10. Trust and Trustees.
11. Administrators-general and official trustees.

1[11A. Administration of Justice; constitution and organisation of all courts, except the Supreme Court and the High Courts.]

12. Evidence and oaths; recognition of laws, public acts and records, and judicial proceedings.
13. Civil procedure, including all matters included in the Code of Civil Procedure at the commencement of this Constitution, limitation and arbitration.
14. Contempt of court, but not including contempt of the Supreme Court.

15. Vagrancy; nomadic and migratory tribes.
16. Lunacy and mental deficiency, including places for the reception or treatment of lunatics and mental deficients.
17. Prevention of cruelty to animals.

17A. Forests.

17B. Protection of wild animals and birds.

18. Adulteration of foodstuffs and other goods.
19. Drugs and poisons, subject to the provisions of entry 59 of List I with respect to opium.
20. Economic and social planning.

20A. Population control and family planning.

21. Commercial and industrial monopolies, combines and trusts.
22. Trade unions; industrial and labour disputes.
23. Social security and social insurance; employment and unemployment.
24. Welfare of labour including conditions of work, provident funds, employers' liability, workmen's compensation, invalidity and old age pensions and maternity benefits.
25. Education, including technical education, medical education and universities, subject to the provisions of entries 63, 64, 65 and 66 of List I; vocational and technical training of labour.]
26. Legal, medical and other professions.
27. Relief and rehabilitation of persons displaced from their original place of residence by reason of the setting up of the Dominions of India and Pakistan.
28. Charities and charitable institutions, charitable and religious endowments and religious institutions.
29. Prevention of the extension from one State to another of infectious or contagious diseases or pests affecting men, animals or plants.
30. Vital statistics including registration of births and deaths.
31. Ports other than those declared by or under law made by Parliament or existing law to be major ports.

32. Shipping and navigation on inland waterways as regards mechanically propelled vessels, and the rule of the road on such waterways, and the carriage of passengers and goods on inland waterways subject to the provisions of List I with respect to national waterways.

1[33. Trade and commerce in, and the production, supply and distribution of,—

  (*a*) the products of any industry where the control of such industry by the Union is declared by Parliament by law to be expedient in the public interest, and imported goods of the same kind as such products;

  (*b*) foodstuffs, including edible oilseeds and oils;

  (*c*) cattle fodder, including oilcakes and other concentrates;

  (*d*) raw cotton, whether ginned or unginned, and cotton seed; and

  (*e*) raw jute.]

2[33A. Weights and measures except establishment of standards.]

34. Price control.

35. Mechanically propelled vehicles including the principles on which taxes on such vehicles are to be levied.

36. Factories.

37. Boilers.

38. Electricity.

39. Newspapers, books and printing presses.

40. Archaeological sites and remains other than those 1[declared by or under law made by Parliament] to be of national importance.

41. Custody, management and disposal of property (including agricultural land) declared by law to be evacuee property.

2[42. Acquisition and requisitioning of property.]

43. Recovery in a State of claims in respect of taxes and other public demands, including arrears of land-revenue and sums recoverable as such arrears, arising outside that State.

44. Stamp duties other than duties or fees collected by means of judicial stamps, but not including rates of stamp duty.

45. Inquiries and statistics for the purposes of any of the matters specified in List II or List III.
46. Jurisdiction and powers of all courts, except the Supreme Court, with respect to any of the matters in this List.
47. Fees in respect of any of the matters in this List, but not including fees taken in any court.

Eleventh Schedule

(Article 243G)
(For the Panchayats)

1. Agriculture, including agricultural extension.
2. Land improvement, implementation of land reforms, land consolidation and soil conservation.
3. Minor irrigation, water management and watershed development.
4. Animal husbandry, dairying and poultry.
5. Fisheries.
6. Social forestry and farm forestry.
7. Minor forest produce.
8. Small scale industries, including food processing industries.
9. Khadi, village and cottage industries.
10. Rural housing.
11. Drinking water.
12. Fuel and fodder.
13. Roads, culverts, bridges, ferries, waterways and other means of communication.
14. Rural electrification, including distribution of electricity.
15. Non-conventional energy sources.
16. Poverty alleviation programme.
17. Education, including primary and secondary schools.
18. Technical training and vocational education.
19. Adult and non-formal education.
20. Libraries.

21. Cultural activities.
22. Markets and fairs.
23. Health and sanitation, including hospitals, primary health centres and dispensaries.
24. Family welfare.
25. Women and child development.
26. Social welfare, including welfare of the handicapped and mentally retarded.
27. Welfare of the weaker sections, and in particular, of the Scheduled Castes and the Scheduled Tribes.
28. Public distribution system.
29. Maintenance of community assets.

Twelfth Schedule

(Article 243W)
(For the Municipalities)

1. Urban planning including town planning.
2. Regulation of land-use and construction of buildings.
3. Planning for economic and social development.
4. Roads and bridges.
5. Water supply for domestic, industrial and commercial purposes.
6. Public health, sanitation conservancy and solid waste management.
7. Fire services.
8. Urban forestry, protection of the environment and promotion of ecological aspects.
9. Safeguarding the interests of weaker sections of society, including the handicapped and mentally retarded.
10. Slum improvement and upgradation.
11. Urban poverty alleviation.
12. Provision of urban amenities and facilities such as parks, gardens, playgrounds.
13. Promotion of cultural, educational and aesthetic aspects.
14. Burials and burial grounds; cremations, cremation grounds; and electric crematoriums.
15. Cattle pounds; prevention of cruelty to animals.
16. Vital statistics including registration of births and deaths.

17. Public amenities including street lighting, parking lots, bus stops and public conveniences.
18. Regulation of slaughter houses and tanneries.

Appendices - 2

Conduct of Government of Business under Article. 166 of the Constitution of India

Art. 166. (1) All executive action of the Government of a State shall be expressed to be taken in the name of the Governor.

(2) Orders and other instruments made and executed in the name of the Governor shall be authenticated in such manner as may be specified in rules to be made by the Governor, and the validity of an order or instrument which is so authenticated shall not be called in question on the ground that it is not an order or instrument made or executed by the Governor.

(3) The Governor shall make rules for the more convenient transaction of the business of the Government of the State, and for the allocation among Ministers of the said business insofar as it is not business with respect to which the Governor is by or under this Constitution to act in his discretion.

Appendices - 2.1

Specimen of a notification under Article 166(3) by a State Government of the Extracts

Rules of Business published by Govt of West Bengal under Article 166(3) of the Constitution of India vide Notification No. 1209A.R. dated 5.6.1964

In exercise of the power conferred by clause (3) of Article 166 of the Constitution of India, and in supersession of all previous rules made in this behalf, the Governor of West Bengal is pleased to make the following rules, namely :

1. These rules may be called the West Bengal Rules of Business.
2. In these rules, unless the context otherwise requires –
   (a) "Article" means an Article of the Constitution of India;
   (b) "Council" means the Council of Ministers constituted under Article 163; and "Cabinet" means the Committee of the Council referred to in rule 11;
   (c) "Secretary" means a Secretary to the Government of the State; and includes – The Chief Secretary, the Additional Chief Secretary, a Special Secretary; an Additional Secretary, a Joint Secretary, a Deputy Secretary, an Under Secretary and an Assistant Secretary;

(d) "Schedule" means the Schedule appended to these rules.

3. The General Clauses Act, 1897, applies for the interpretation of these rules as it applies for the interpretation of a Central Act.

....

Part I. – Allocation and Disposal of Business

4. The business of the Government shall be transacted in the departments specified in the First Schedule and shall be classified and distributed between those departments as laid down therein.

5. The Governor shall, on the advice of the Chief Minister, allot among the Ministers the business of the Government by assigning one or more departments to the charge of a Minister:

Provided that nothing in this rule shall prevent the assigning of one department to the charge of more than one Minister:

....

First Schedule

[See rule 4]

....

Allocation of business among departments

Departments

I. Home Department

II. Finance Department

....

V. Agriculture

VIII. Department of Commerce and Industries

....

XI. Health and Family Welfare Department

....

....

1. "List I", "List II" and "List III" mean List I, List II and List III, respectively of the Seventh Schedule to the Constitution of India.
2. The business falling to each department is set forth in this schedule in three parts –

   Part I defines the functions of the department.

   Part II indicates, primarily by reference to List II and List III, the area within the sphere of the State's executive authority and power to make laws, within which the department exercise its functions. Items falling in List III are printed in italics.

   Part III indicates, by reference to List I, the area within the sphere of the Union executive authority and power to make laws, within which the department transact such business as falls to the State Government (whether this be discharging agency functions or functions entrusted to it or merely furnishing advice or information by way of correspondence).

....

Department of Municipal Affairs

Part I

Promotion of local self-government and financing, regulation and inspection of authorities established for local self-government and for urban development other than the Board of Trustees for the improvement of Calcutta and the Board of Trustees for the improvement of Howrah.

Part II

2. Local government, that is to say, the constitution and powers of municipal corporations, district boards and other local authorities for the purpose of local self-government referred to in entry 5 of List II, excluding village administration and improvement trusts.

5. Inquires and statistics for the purposes of any of the matters specified in List II or List III with which the department is concerned (entry 45 of List III).
6. Tolls in respect of any matter with which the department is concerned (entry 59 of List II).
11. Communications, that is to say, roads, bridges, ferries and other means of communications (not specified in List I) with which local bodies are concerned, municipal tramways (entry 13 of List II).
13. Taxes on lands and buildings (entry 49 of List II).
14. Taxes on professions, trades, callings and employment (entry 60 of List II).
15. Taxes on animals and boats (entry 58 of List II).
16. Taxes on the entry of goods into a local area for consumption, use or sale therein (entry 52 of List II).
17. Taxes on vehicles, other than mechanically propelled vehicles, suitable for use on roads subject to the provisions of entry 35 of List III (entry 57 of List II).

....

Part III

2. Inquiries, surveys and statistics for the purpose of any of the matters in List I with which the department is concerned (entry 94 of List I).

....

Department of Panchayat and Rural Development
Part I

1. Constitution and Organisation of Panchayats as institutions of self-government at the village, intermediate and district levels with necessary powers and authority.
2. Devolution of powers and responsibilities upon Panchayats at the appropriate level for preparation of plan for economic development and social justice and implementation of assigned schemes including those related to the matters listed in the Eleventh Schedule.

5. Local development works and any other development work in rural areas not specifically assigned to any other department.
6. Coordination between departments and agencies of the State Government and the Panchayats concerned with the implementation of schemes for economic development and social justice.

....

Part II

3. Local Government, that is to say, the constitution and powers of Panchayats at different levels for the purpose of local self-government or Village administration (entry 5 of List II).
5. Communications, that is to say, roads, bridges, ferries and other means of communications (not specified in List I) with which the Panchayats are concerned (entry 13 of List II).
7. Taxes on agricultural income with which the Panchayats are concerned (entry 46 of List II).
8. Taxes of lands and buildings with which the Panchayats are concerned (entry 49 of List II).
9. Taxes on vehicles, whether mechanically propelled or not, suitable for use on roads so far as the Panchayats are concerned (entry 57 of List II).
11. Tolls in respect of any matter with which the department is concerned (entry 59 of List II).
16. Inquiries and statistics for the purpose of any of the matters specified in List II or List III (entry 45 of List III).
18. Social, planning, including Community Development Projects, with which the department is concerned (entry 20 of List III).

....

Part III

2. Inquiries, surveys and statistics for the purpose of any of the matters in List I with which the department is concerned (entry 94 of List I).

....

Appendices - 2.2

State-Kerala

FUNCTIONS ASSIGNED TO THE PANCHAYAT RAJ INSTITUTIONS

VILLAGE PANCHAYATS

A. Mandatory functions of Village Panchayats

1. Regulation of building construction
2. Protection of public land from encroachment
3. Protection of traditional drinking water sources
4. Presentation of ponds and other water bodies
5. Maintenance of water-ways and canals under their charge
6. Collection and disposal of solid waste and control of liquid waste disposal
7. Storm water drainage
8. Maintenance of environmental hygiene
9. Management of markets
10. Vector control
11. Regulation of slaughtering of animals and sale of meat fish and other perishable food items
12. Regulation of eating establishments
13. Prevention of food adulteration
14. Maintenance of roads and other public assets
15. Street lighting and their maintenance
16. Immunisation
17. Carrying into effect national and State level strategies and programmes for disease prevention and control

18. Opening and maintenance of burial and burning grounds.
19. Licensing of dangerous and offensive trades
20. Registration of births and deaths
21. Provide bathing and washing ghats
22. Provide of ferries
23. Provide parking space for vehicles
24. Provide waiting-sheds for travellers
25. Provide toilet facilities in public places
26. Regulate conduct of fairs and festivals
27. Licensing of pet dogs and destroying stray dogs

B. General functions

1. Collection and updating of essential statistics.
2. Organising voluntary labour and contribution for community works.
3. Carrying out campaigns for thrift.
4. Awareness building on control of social evils like drinking, consumption of narcotics, dowry and abuse of women and children.
5. Ensuring maximum people's participation in all stages of development.
6. Organising relief during natural calamities.
7. Inculcating environmental awareness and motivating local action for environmental upgradation.
8. Promoting co-operatives.
9. Enhancing communal harmony
10. Mobilizing local resources in cash and in kind, including free surrender of land for development purposes.
11. Spreading legal awareness among the weaker sections.
12. Campaigning against economic crimes
13. Organising neighbourhood groups and self-help groups with focus on the poor.
14. Awareness building on civic duties

C. Sector-wise distribution of responsibilities

(i) *Agriculture*

1. Bring into cultivation waste lands and marginal lands
2. Bring about an optimum utilisation of land
3. Soil conservation
4. Production of organic manure
5. Establishment of nurseries
6. Promotion of co-operative and group farming
7. Organising self-help groups among cultivators
8. Promotion of horticulture and vegetable cultivation.
9. Fodder development
10. Plant protection
11. Seed production
12. Farm mechanisation
13. Management of Krishi Bhavans

(ii) *Animal Husbandry and Dairy*

1. Cattle improvement programmes
2. Dairy farming
3. Poultry farming, bee keeping, piggery development, goat rearing, rabbit rearing
4. Running or veterinary dispensaries
5. Running of ICDP sub-centres
6. Preventive health programmes for animals
7. Prevention of cruelty to animals
8. Fertility improvement programmes
9. Control of diseases of animal origin

(iii) *Minor Irrigation*

All minor irrigation schemes within the area of a Village Panchayat.

1. All micro irrigation schemes
2. Water conservation

(iv) *Fisheries*

1. Development of fisheries in ponds and fresh water and brackish water fish culture, mari culture
2. Fish seed production and distribution

3. Distribution of fishing implements
4. Fish marketing assistance
5. Provision of basic minimum services for the families of fishermen
6. Welfare schemes for fishermen

(v) *Social Forestry*

1. Raising of fodder, fuel and fruit trees
2. Organising campaigns for tree planting and environmental awareness
3. Afforestation of waste lands

(vi) *Small Scale Industries*

1. Promotion of cottage and village industries
2. Promotion of handicrafts
3. Promotion of traditional and mini industries

(vii) *Housing*

1. Identification of homeless people and poramboke dwellers and provide house sites and houses
2. Implementation of rural housing programmes
3. Implementation of shelter upgradation programmes

(viii) *Water Supply*

1. Running of water supply schemes covering one village panchayat
2. Setting up of water supply schemes covering one village panchayat

(ix) *Electricity and Energy*

1. Street lighting
2. Promotion of Bio-gas

(x) *Education*

1. Management of Government pre-primary schools and Government primary schools
2. Literacy programmes

(xi) Public Works

1. Construction and maintenance of village roads within the village panchayat
2. Construction of buildings for institutions transferred

(xii) Public Health and Sanitation

1. Management of dispensaries and primary health centres and sub-centres (in all systems of medicine)
2. Management of child welfare centres and maternity homes
3. Immunization and other preventive measures
4. Family Welfare
5. Sanitation

(xiii) Social Welfare

1. Running of anganwadies
2. Sanctioning and distribution of pensions to destitute widows, handicapped and agricultural labourers
3. Sanctioning and distribution of unemployment assistance
4. Sanctioning of assistance for marriage of the daughters of widows
5. Management of group insurance scheme for the poor

(xiv) Poverty Alleviation

1. Identification of the poor
2. Self employment and group employment schemes for the poor especially women
3. Providing community assets of continuing benefit to the poor

(xv) Scheduled Castes and Scheduled Tribes Development

1. Beneficiary oriented schemes under SCP and TSP
2. Management of nursery school for Scheduled Castes and Scheduled Tribes

3. Provision of basic amenities in Scheduled Castes and Scheduled Tribes habitats
4. Assistant to Scheduled Castes and Scheduled Tribes students
5. Discretionary assistance to Scheduled Castes and Scheduled Tribes in need

(xvi) Sports and Cultural Affairs

1. Construction of play grounds

(xvii) Public Distribution System

1. Examination of complaints against the public distribution system and taking of remedial measures
2. Organisation of campaigns against weights and measures offences
3. General supervision and guidance of ration shops and maveli stores and other public distribution centres and if necessary starting new public distribution centres

(xviii) Natural Calamities Relief

1. Management of relief centres
2. Organisation of relief works (Repair works to assets will be divided and carried out by the Panchayat in charge of the assets)

(xix) Co-Operatives

1. Organisation of co-operatives within the jurisdiction of the Panchayat
2. Payment of Government grants and subsidies within the jurisdiction

II. BLOCK PANCHAYATS

A. General functions

1. Pool technical expertise both Government and non-government at the Block level

2. Provide technical services to Village Panchayats
3. Prepare plans after taking into account the plans of Village Panchayat to avoid duplication and provide the backward and forward linkages

B. Sector-wise distribution of responsibilities

(i) Agriculture

1. Farmers' training for the programmes implemented at the village level
2. Arrangements of agricultural inputs required for schemes at the village level
3. Conduct of agricultural exhibitions
4. Integrated watershed management in watersheds falling within Block Panchayat area
5. Mobilize agricultural credit
6. Sericulture

(ii) Animal Husbandry and Dairy

1. Running of Veterinary Polyclinics and Regional Artificial Insemination Centres
2. Provide speciality services in Animal Husbandry
3. Conduct cattle and poultry shows

(iii) Minor Irrigation

All lift irrigation schemes and minor irrigation schemes covering more than one village Panchayat

(iv) Fisheries

Development of traditional landing centres

(v) Small Scale Industries

1. Setting up of mini industrial estates
2. Promotion of industries with investment limit of one-third of SSI
3. Self employment schemes in industrial sector

(vi) Housing

1. Popularisation of low cost housing
2. Promotion of housing co-operative societies

(vii) Electricity and Energy

Promotion of non-conventional energy sources

(viii) Education

Management of Industrial Training Institutes

(ix) Public Works

1. Construction and maintenance of all village roads connecting more than one Village Panchayat and other District Roads within the block Panchayat
2. Construction of buildings for institutions transferred

(x) Public Health and Sanitation

Management of community health centres and taluk hospitals within the Block Panchayat area in all systems of medicine

(xi) Social Welfare

Management of ICDS

(xii) Poverty Alleviation

1. Planning and implementation of Employment Assurance Schemes in co-ordination with the Village Panchayats
2. Skill upgradation of the poor for self employment and wage employment for people below poverty line

(xiii) Scheduled Castes and Scheduled Tribes Development

1. Management of pre-matric hostels
2. Promoting Scheduled Castes and Scheduled Tribes Co-operatives

(xiv) Co-operatives

1. Organisation of co-operatives within the jurisdiction of Block Panchayat
2. Payment of Government grants and subsidies within the jurisdiction

III. DISTRICT PANCHAYATS

A. General Functions

1. Mobilize the technical expertise available from Government and non-government institutions.
2. Provide technical service to the Block Panchayats and Village Panchayats and the Municipalities.
3. Prepare plans after taking into account the plans of the Village Panchayats and Block Panchayats to avoid duplication and to provide backward and forward linkage.

B. Sector-wise Distribution of Responsibilities

(i) Agriculture

1. Running of agricultural farms other than regional farms and research centres and establishment of new farms
2. Integrated watershed management in watersheds covering more than one Block Panchayat area
3. Provision of agricultural inputs
4. Soil testing
5. Pest control
6. Marketing of agricultural produce
7. Cultivation of ornamental plants
8. Promotion of agricultural co-operatives
9. Promotion of commercial crops
10. Biotechnology applications
11. Field trials and pilot projects to popularise innovation
12. Locally appropriate research and development

(ii) *Animal Husbandry and Dairy*

1. Management of district level veterinary hospitals and laboratories
2. Management of dairy extension service units
3. Promotion of milk co-operatives
4. Management of farms other than regional farms, breeding farms and research centres
5. District level training
6. Implementation of disease prevention programmes
7. Field trials and pilot projects on innovative practices
8. Locally relevant research and development

(iii) *Minor Irrigation*

1. Development of ground water resources
2. Construction and maintenance of minor irrigation schemes covering more than one Block Panchayat
3. Command area development

(iv) *Fisheries*

1. Arrangements for marketing of fish
2. Management of Fish Farm Development Agency
3. Management of district level hatcheries, net making units, fish markets, feed mills, ice plants and cold storages
4. Management of fisheries schools
5. Introduction of new technologies
6. Provide inputs required for fishermen
7. Promotion of fishermen's co-operatives

(v) *Small Scale Industries*

1. Management of District Industries Centre
2. Promotion of small scale industries
3. Setting up of industrial estates
4. Arranging exhibitions for sale of products
5. Entrepreneur development programmes
6. Marketing of products

7. Training
8. Input service and common facility centres
9. Industrial development credit planning

(vi) Housing

1. Housing complex and infrastructure development
2. Mobilizing housing finance

(vii) Water Supply

1. Running of water supply schemes covering more than one Village Panchayat
2. Taking up of water supply schemes covering more than one Village Panchayat

(viii) Electricity and Energy

1. aking up of micro-hydel projects
2. Determining priority areas for extension of electricity

(ix) Education

1. Management of Government high schools (including LP section and UP section attached to high schools)
2. Management of Government higher secondary schools
3. Management of Government technical schools
4. Management of vocational training centres and polytechnics
5. Management of vocational Higher Secondary schools
6. Management of District Institute for Education and Training
7. Co-ordinate centrally and State sponsored programmes related to education

(x) Public Works

1. Construction and maintenance of all district roads other than State Highways, National Highways and Major District Roads

2. Construction of buildings for institutions transferred

(xi) Public Health and Sanitation

1. Management of district hospital in all systems of medicine
2. Setting up of centres for care of special categories of disabled and mentally ill people
3. Co-ordination of centrally and State Sponsored programme at the district level

(xii) Social Welfare

1. Payment of grants to orphanages
2. Starting of welfare institutions for the disabled, destitutes etc

(xiii) Poverty Alleviation

Providing infrastructure for self-employment programmes.

(xiv) Scheduled Castes and Scheduled Tribes Development

1. Management of post matric hostels
2. Management of vocational training centres for Scheduled Castes and Scheduled Tribes

(xv) Sports and Cultural Affairs

Construction of stadiums

(xvi) Co-Operatives

1. Organisation of co-operatives within the jurisdiction of District Panchayats.
2. Payment of Government grants and subsidies to co-operatives within the jurisdiction.

FUNCTIONS OF URBAL LOCAL GOVERNMENTS

A. Mandatory Functions

1. Regulating building construction
2. Protection of public land from encroachment

3. Conservation of traditional drinking water sources
4. Preservation of ponds and other water tanks
5. Maintenance of waterways and canals under the control of the Municipality
6. Collection and disposal of solid waste and regulation of disposal of liquid waste
7. Storm water drainage
8. Maintenance of environmental hygiene
9. Management of public markets
10. Vector control
11. Regulation of slaughtering of animals and sale of meat, fish and other easily perishable food stuffs etc
12. Control of eating houses
13. Prevention of food adulteration
14. Maintenance of roads and other public properties
15. Street lighting and its maintenance
16. Adopt immunisation measures
17. Effective implementation of National and State Level strategies and programmes for prevention and control of diseases
18. Establishment and maintenance of burial and burning grounds
19. Issue of licences to dangerous and offensive trades and industries
20. Registration of births and deaths
21. Providing bathing and washing ghats
22. Arranging ferries
23. Providing parking spaces for vehicles
24. Construction of waiting sheds for travellers
25. Providing toilet facilities and bathing ghats at public places
26. Regulating the conduct of fairs and festivals
27. Issue licence to domestic dogs and destroy stray dogs
28. Providing basic facilities in slum areas
29. Amenities including foot path and road crossing facilities for pedestrains

30. Preparation of detailed town planning and Action plan for implementation in a phased manner

B. General Functions

1. Collection and updating of essential statistics
2. Organising voluntary workers and make them participate in collective activities
3. Organise campaign for thrift
4. Awareness building against social evils like drinking, consumption of narcotics, dowry and abuse of women and children
5. Ensuring maximum people's participation in all stages of development
6. Organise relief activities during natural calamities
7. Inculcating environmental awareness and motivating local action for its upgradation
8. Development of Co-operative Sector
9. Promoting communal harmony
10. Mobilizing local resources in cash or in kind including free surrender of Land for developmental purpose
11. Propagating legal awareness among the weaker sections
12. Campaign against economic offenses
13. Organizing neighbourhood groups and self help groups with focus on the poor
14. Awareness building on civil duties

C. Sector-wise Distribution of Functions

(i) Agriculture

1. Bring into cultivation barren land and surrounding land
2. Ensure optimum utilization of land
3. Soil Conservation
4. Production of organic manure
5. Establishment of nurseries
6. Promotion of Co-operative group farming
7. Organizing self-help groups among farmers
8. Promotion of horticulture and vegetable cultivation

9. Implementation of fodder crop development
10. Encourage plant protection activities
11. Development of seed production
12. Implementation of farm mechanisation
13. Running of Krishi Bhavans
14. Organize Agricultural exhibitions

(ii) Animal Husbandry and Dairy Farming

1. Implementation of cattle improvement programmes
2. Increase the production of milk
3. Poultry farming, bee keeping, piggery development, goat rearing and rabbit rearing
4. Running of veterinary hospitals
5. Running of I.C.D.P. sub-centres
6. Formulation and implementation of preventive-health programme for animals
7. Prevention of cruelty to animals
8. Implementation of fertility improvement programmes
9. Control of animal origin disease
10. Running of veterinary poly-clinics and Regional Artificial Insemination Centres
11. Providing of speciality services in animal husbandry
12. Conduct cattle poultry shows

(iii) Minor Irrigation

1. Implementation and maintenance of all minor and lift irrigation projects within the Municipal areas
2. Implementation and maintenance of all micro-irrigation projects
3. Carry out conservation of water
4. Implementation of ground water resources development

(iv) Fisheries

1. Implementation of pici-culture in ponds, fresh water and brackish in water and development of marine products
2. Promotion of fish seed production and distribution
3. Distribution of fishing implements
4. Providing assistance for fish marketing

5. Providing of minimum basic services for fishermen families
6. Implementation of fishermen welfare scheme
7. Development of traditional landing centres
8. Administrative control of fisheries schools

(v) *Social Forestry*

1. Growing of trees for fodder or fuel and growing of fruit trees
2. Organize campaign for planting of trees and environmental awareness
3. Afforestation of waste land

(vi) *Small Scale Industries*

1. Promotion of cottage-village industries
2. Promotion of handicrafts
3. Promotion of traditional and mini industries
4. Establishment of Mini Industrial Estates
5. Encourage the industries with investment of one-third of SSI limit
6. Formulate and implement self employment schemes in Industrial Sector
7. Promotion of small scale industries
8. Implementation of the entrepreneur development programmes

(vii) *Housing*

1. Identify the homeless and purampoke dwellers and to provide house sites and houses
2. Implementing housing programmes
3. Implementing the shelter rejuvenation programmes
4. Popularizing the low-cost housing
5. Encourage housing co-operative societies
6. Implement the development of housing complex and infrastructure
7. Mobilize fund necessary for housing

(viii) Water Supply

1. Maintain water supply schemes within the respective Municipal area
2. Arrange water supply schemes within the respective Municipalities

(ix) Electricity and Energy

1. Install street lights
2. Encourage the consumption of bio-gass
3. Promote non-conventional energy sources

(x) Education

1. Run the Government pre-primary schools, primary schools and high schools
2. Implement literary programmes
3. Run the Government Industrial Training Centres in the Municipal area
4. Run the Government Higher Secondary Schools in the Municipal area
5. Run the Government Technical Schools in the Municipal area
6. Run the Government Vocational Training Centres and Polytechnics in the Municipal area
7. Run the Government Vocational Higher Secondary Schools in the Municipal area.

Source: 62 Kerala – A Case Study of Classical Democratic Decentralization, Kila

Appendices - 2.3

State: West Bengal

PROVISIONS UNDER THE WEST BENGAL PANCHAYAT ACT 1973 vis-à-vis ELEVENTH SCHEDULE OF THE CONSTITUTION

Sl. no	*Eleventh Schedule*	*Gram Panchayat*			*Panchayat Samiti*		*Zilla Parishad*	
		Obligatory	*If assigned*	*Discretionary*	*Optional*	*Otherwise*	*Optional*	*Otherwise*
(1)	*(2)*	*(3)*	*(4)*	*(5)*	*(6)*	*(7)*	*(8)*	*(9)*
1.	Agriculture, including Agricultural Extension		20(1)(e)	21(1)(f) 21(1)(g)	109(1)(a)(i)		153 (a)(i)	
2.	Land improvement, implementation of land reforms, land consolidation and soil conservation		20 (1) (i) 20(1) (n) 20(i) (l)		109(1)(a)(i)		153 (a)(i)	
3.	Minor irrigation, water management and watershed development		20(1) (d)	21 (c)	109(1)(a)(i)		153 (a)(i)	
4.	Animal husbandry, dairying and poultry		20 (1) (h)	21 (iL)	109(i)(a)(i)		153 (a)(i)	
5.	Fisheries		21 (i2)		109(f)(a)(i)		153 (a)(i)	
6.	Social Forestry and Farm Forestry		20(i) (k)	21 (b)	109(f)(a)(i)		153 (a)(i)	
7.	Minor forest produce		20(i) (q)				153 (a)(i)	

(Contd.)

(Contd. Appendices 2.3)

Sl. no	Eleventh Schedule	Gram Panchayat			Panchayat Samiti		Zilla Parishad	
		Obliga-tory	*If assigned*	*Discre-tionary*	*Optional*	*Other-wise*	*Optional*	*Other-wise*
(1)	*(2)*	*(3)*	*(4)*	*(5)*	*(6)*	*(7)*	*(8)*	*(9)*
8.	Small Scale industries including food processing industries			21 (i)			153 (a)(i)	
9.	Khadi, village and cottage industries			21 (i)			153 (a)(i)	
10.	Rural Housing		20(i) (r)			***	153 (a)(i)	***
11.	Drinking water	19 (2) (c)			109(f)(a)(i)		*153 (a)(i)	
12.	Fuel and fodder		20(i) (e)		109(f)(a)(i)		153 (a)(i)	
13.	Roads, culverts, bridges, ferries, waterways and other means of communication				109 (1) (a)(i)		153 (a)(i) **	
14.	Rural electrification, including distribution of electricity		20(1) (s)	21 (a)	109 (1) (a)(i)		153 (a)(i)	
15.	Non-conventional energy sources		20(i) (t)		109 (1) (a)(i)	***	153 (a)(i)	***
16.	Poverty alleviation programme		***	21 (I 3)				

(Contd.)

(Contd. Appendices 2.3)

Sl. no	*Eleventh Schedule*	*Gram Panchayat*			*Panchayat Samiti*		*Zilla Parishad*	
		Obligatory	*If assigned*	*Discretionary*	*Optional*	*Otherwise*	*Optional*	*Otherwise*
(1)	*(2)*	*(3)*	*(4)*	*(5)*	*(6)*	*(7)*	*(8)*	*(9)*
17.	Education including primary and secondary schools		20(1) (a)		10(1) (a)(i)		153(a)(i)	
18.	Technical training and vocational education		20(1) (a)				153(a)(i)	
19.	Adult and non-formal education		20(1) (a)		109(1)(a)(i)		153(a)(i)	
20.	Libraries			21 (o)				
21.	Cultural activities			21(p 1)				
22.	Markets and fairs			21 (e)			153(a)(i)	
23.	Health and Sanitation including hospitals, primary health centres, and dispensaries	19 (2) a 19 (2) b		21 (h) 21 (m) 21(n)	109(1)(a)(i)			
24.	Family Welfare		20 (1) b					

(Contd.)

(Contd. Appendices 2.3)

Sl. No	*Eleventh Schedule*	*Gram Panchayat*			*Panchayat Samiti*		*Zilla Parishad*	
		Obligatory	*If assigned*	*Discretionary*	*Optional*	*Otherwise*	*Optional*	*Otherwise*
(1)	*(2)*	*(3)*	*(4)*	*(5)*	*(6)*	*(7)*	*(8)*	*(9)*
25.	Women & Child Development		20 (1) u		109(1)(a)(i)		153(a)(i)	
26.	Social welfare including welfare of the handicapped and mentally retarded		20 (i) f	21 (p 2)	109(1)(a)(i)		153(a)(i)	
27.	Welfare of the weaker sections and in particular of the Scheduled Castes and Scheduled Tribes			21 (p 3)				
28.	Public Distribution System			21 (p 4)				
29.	Maintenance of community assets			21 (p 5)	109 (iii)		153(a)(i)	

* Water supply but not drinking water

** Communications only

*** Not under any provision of the West Bengal Panchayat Act, 1973 but under Notification No. 3369 PN/)/4P-1/05, dated 25.2.2006

Source: Separate Report on Third State Finance Commission,West Bengal by Dr. B.P. Syam Roy, Member Third State Finance Commission,West Bengal

Appendices - 2.4

State: West Bengal

Provisions of the West Bengal Municipal Act 1993 vis-à-vis Twelfth Schedule of the Constitution

Twelfth Schedule		*Provisions under the West Bengal Municipal Act, 1993*		
		Obligatory functions Section 63	*Discretionary functions Section 64*	*Transfer of functions of State Government Section 65*
1.	Urban Planning including town planning.	63(3)		65(2)a, 65(2)b
2.	Regulation of land-use and construction of buildings.	63(3)e, 63(4)a, 63(4)b, 63(4)c, 63(4)e, 63(4)i		
3.	Planning for economic and social development.	63(4)g, 63(4)h, 63(4)j, 63(4)k, 63(4)n	64(1)f, 64(1)h, 64(3)c, 64(3)f, 64(4)b, 64(4)c, 64(4)g, 64(5)a, 64(5)c, 64(5)e, 64(5)g, 64(5)h, 64(5)i, 64(5)l	65(2)g, 65(2)i

(Contd.)

(Contd. Appendices 2.4)

	Twelfth Schedule	*Provisions under the West Bengal Municipal Act, 1993*		
		Obligatory functions Section 63	*Discretionary functions Section 64*	*Transfer of functions of State Government Section 65*
4.	Water supply for domestic, industrial and commercial purposes.	63(1)a, 63(1)j, 63(2)f, 63(2)g	Sec. 64(3)b, 64(4)f	65(2)c
5.	Public health, sanitation conservancy and solid waste management.	63(1)b, 63(1)c, 63(2)a, 63(2)b, 63(2)c, 63(2)d, 63(2)i, 63(2)j, 63(2)k, 63(2)l, 63(2)m	64(2)e, 64(3)d, 64(3)g, 64(4)f	65(2)c, 65(2)f
6.	Fire services.	63(2)m		65(2)m
7.	Urban forestry, protection of the environment and promotion of ecological aspects.	63(1)g, 63(2)d, 63(4)l	64(3)e, 64(5)d	65(2)p, 65(2)q
8.	Safeguarding the interests of weaker sections of society, including the handicapped and mentally retarded.		64(1)a, 64(1)b, 64(1)c, 64(1)d, 64(1)g, 64(5)b	65(2)g, 65(2)o

(Contd.)

(Contd. Appendices 2.4)

Twelfth Schedule		*Provisions under the West Bengal Municipal Act, 1993*		
		Obligatory functions Section 63	*Discretionary functions Section 64*	*Transfer of functions of State Government Section 65*
9.	Urban poverty alleviation.		64(5)j	65(2)e, 65(2)j
10.	Provision of urban amenities and facilities such as parks, gardens, playgrounds.	63(3)h, 63(3)l	64(1)b, 64(2)a	65(2)n
11.	Promotion of cultural, educational and aesthetic aspects.	63(1)i, 63(3)k	64(2)a, 64(2)b, 64(2)c, 64(2)d, 64(2)f, 64(4)d, 64(5)f	65(2)j, 65(2)n
12.	Burials and burial grounds; cremations, cremation grounds and electric crematoriums.	63(2)h		
13.	Cattle pounds; prevention of cruelty to animals.		64(3)a	

(Contd.)

(Contd. Appendices 2.4)

	Twelfth Schedule	*Provisions under the West Bengal Municipal Act,1993*		
		Obligatory functions Section 63	*Discretionary functions Section 64*	*Transfer of functions of State Government Section 65*
17.	Public amenities including street lighting, parking lots, bus stops and public conveniences.	Sec. 63(1)f	64(1)b, 64(3)g, 64(4)c, 64(4)d, 64(4)e	65(2)d, 65(2)k, 65(2)l
18.	Regulation of slaughter houses and tanneries.	Sec. 63(1)h		

Source: Separate Report on Third State Finance Commission,West Bengal by Dr.B.P.Syam Roy, Member Third State Finance Commission,West Bengal

Appendices - 3

Guidelines for District Plans in the Eleventh Five Year Plan by the Planning Commission

(I) Introduction

The need for integrated local area plans, based on specific endowments and needs of each area, was stressed from the beginning of planned development in1950s. However, despite several reports and studies, there were only sporadic efforts and isolated cases of such planning. Development was mostly done through sectoral schemes and programmes of a uniform nature, resulting in limited outcomes and wastage of resources. The constitution 73rd and 74th Amendments mandated local planning at the Village Panchayat, Intermediate Panchayats and District Panchayat levels as well as in urban local governments and their consolidation into a District Plan in each district. Though more than fourteen years have gone by since the constitutional mandate was brought into effect, there has been little progress except in very few states.It has been decided that the 'district plan process' should be an integral part of the process of preparation of state's Eleventh Five Year Plan (2007-2012) and the annual plan 2007-2008. With this in view, the Ministry of Panchayati Raj constituted an Expert Group in 2005, in consultation with the Planning Commission.

The Report of the Expert Group on planning at the grassroots level was presented to government in March 2006. It has been accepted by the Ministry of Panchayati Raj and the Planning Commission and was circulated the States in April-May 2006. Attention is drawn to Chapter 3 of the Report.

This circular deals with the further steps to be taken as part of the preparation of the states' draft Eleventh Five Year Plan/Annual Plan 2007-2008, proposals.

(II) District Planning

District Planning is the process of preparing an integrated plan for the local government sector in a district taking into account the resources (natural, human and financial) available and covering the sectoral activities and schemes assigned to the district level and below and those implemented through local governments in a state.

The document that embodies this statement of resources and their allocation for various purposes is known as the District Plan. It would essentially have three aspects namely:

1. Plan to be prepared by the Rural Local Bodies for the activities assigned to them and the national/state schemes implemented by them with their own resources and those earmarked for these purposes;
2. Plan to be prepared by the Urban Local Bodies for the activities assigned to them and the national/state schemes implemented by them with their own resources and those earmarked for these purposes;
3. Physical integration of the plans of Rural and Urban Local Bodies with the elements of the State Plan that are physically implemented within the geographical confines of the district.

All the three aspects would be considered and consolidated by the District Planning Committee (DPC) into a District Plan. Quite obviously, the District Plan cannot be prepared in isolation, and must take into account and respond to the expected activities of the non government sector of the local economy. Important among these would be:

1. Plan emerging from activities of people's groups like SHGs, Co-operatives etc.
2. Plan emerging from the financial institutions like the local branch (es) of Commercial Banks (both in the public and the private sector), NABARD, Co-operative Banks and the like.
3. Plans of International Non-Governmental Organizations (INGOs)/NGOS and Bilateral Agencies operating in the District.
4. Plans of other private agents that would either have an impact on the activities of the government or would need the government to respond to those developments insofar as its own areas of functioning/service delivery are concerned.

(III) Steps to be taken at State Level

The State Governments (State Planning Commission/ Board/Department) may take urgent steps for the following, if not already done:-

1. Complete the assignment of Activities to be undertaken by different levels of local governments;
2. Form District Planning Committees (DPC) as envisaged in the constitution, that is, with 80 per cent members being elected from the elected members of the Panchayat and urban local governments in each district and the remaining 20 per cent being nominated by the state governments; preferably with experts.
3. Issue guidelines to the DPC and local governments generally on the lines indicated in Section IV below;
4. Decide on the formula for distribution of local government component of the state plan and indicate the broad order of resources that would be available to different levels (and therefore to each local government) over the five years/one year (2007-08) from the state plan – this would be sector-wise as well as untied;
5. Indicate the resources that would broadly be available to each local government from central sources through

centrally sponsored schemes, special allocations, including those by Finance Commissions, etc;

6. Prepare the Draft District Plans and after vetting, present a summary of District Plans, in the format indicated in Section IV, along with State Plan proposals for the Eleventh Five Year Plan/Annual Plan 2007-08.

(IV) Preparation of District Plan

In the preparation of the draft district plan, the various steps detailed in Chapter 3 of the Report of the Expert Group on Planning at the Grassroots Level may be generally followed. (Provided as Annexure-I). The present state of development and the resource endowment including capability vary widely across states. It is not necessary to wait for perfection or latest technology to get started with the process. Separate steps may be taken to improve internal capabilities.

The following steps are suggested:

1. The available data may be put together for each local government. The state government agencies, the departments and the district statistical organizations (central and state) should assist them in this. Some of the essential items of data are listed in the suggested form at Annexure-II.
2. Based on the data, a vision document for 10 to 15 years is to be prepared by the district and for each local government based on a participatory assessment. The DPC may hold formal interactions with local governments and other key stakeholders on this and then finalize it. The document should clearly identify the key reasons for backwardness/ development shortcomings and address issues impeding development. It will cover:
   - Agriculture and allied sectors (as relevant)
   - Availability and development of water sources
   - Industries – especially traditional, small industries including food processing
   - Infrastructure including power

- Drinking water and sanitation
- Literacy, school education
- Health and medical facilities
- Poverty reduction and basic needs
- Gender and children
- Social Justice – SC/ST, Persons with disability etc.

3. To assist the DPC in preparing the vision document (and subsequently to vet the draft plan proposals), a Technical Support Group may be constituted in each district. It may consist of departmental officers (where available) mandated and nominated for the purpose in addition to their duties or retired persons locally available or a local academic institution or established NGO with a proven record - Similarly, technical support as appropriate, may be organized for the urban areas, Intermediate Panchayats and Village Panchayats.
4. If undertaken in a campaign mode, the preparation of vision document can be completed in two months' time.
5. Further, if District is to be the economic unit for planning exercise, the scope of vision document could be expanded to include areas of comparative advantage of each district (availability of technical institutions, BPO, tourism, agro-industry etc.), which would be the basis for attracting private investment.
6. Based on the vision document/s and following the same participatory process, the needs may be prioritized and goals set for a five-year period for a draft five year plan in the manner indicated below:
   (a) The draft plan preparation should start at the Gram Sabha level. The Gram Panchayat may finalize its Plan based on priorities emerging from the Gram Sabha and give suggestions for the Intermediate Panchayat. Projects and activities which can be implemented at the Gram Panchayat Level should be included as "Gram Panchayat Plan". Those projects and activities which can be implemented only in more than one Gram

Panchayat, will be forwarded to the Intermediate Panchayats to be considered for inclusion into the "Intermediate Panchayat Plan". The Gram Panchayat Plans should also provide an estimate of the community contribution that can be mobilized for the purpose of implementing the development plan.

(b) Based on these suggestions received from Gram Panchayats and its own priorities the Intermediate Panchayat should finalize its Plan.Projects and activities which can be implemented at the Intermediate Panchayat Level should be included as "Intermediate Panchayat Plan". Those projects and activities which need to be implemented in more than one intermediate Panchayat will be forwarded to the District Panchayat to be considered for inclusion into the "District Panchayat Plan".

(c) Based on the Gram Panchayat Plans, the Intermediate Panchayat Plans and District Panchayat Plans, the District Planning Committee shall finalize the District Plan for the District.

(d) A similar exercise may be undertaken in Urban Local Governments. Each local government may be asked to give separate suggestions for inclusion in the Departmental components of the District Plan.

7. The time limit for different steps, in para 6 above, needs to be indicated. Similarly, time frame for integrating District Plans with State Plans also needs to be indicated in view of limited time available for the beginning of Eleventh Five Year Plan.

8. The draft plan proposals of each local government should be in accordance with the approved Activity assignment and the centrally sponsored flag-ship and related programmes (as and where applicable).

9. The draft plan proposals will cover the sectors mentioned in (2) above and will indicate the expected outcomes in terms of production, employment, infrastructure and human development.

10. While preparing the draft plan in accordance with (6), (7), (8) and (9) above, the concerned local government will take into account the district component of the departmental plans as also the Centrally Sponsored Schemes and the Externally Aided Projects that have been assigned to it for implementation. In addition, the physical integration of the District Plan with the elements of the State Plan that are being implemented in the geographical area of the district would need to be given close attention. The resources and outlays in respect of these items of State Plan located in the district (but not implemented through the local bodies) would not, however, be included in the Plan Resources and outlays of the Local Bodies.

11. The local government component of the District Plan would emerge out of the resource envelope containing the following sources of funds:-
    (a) Own resources available for development
    (b) Transfers by State Finance Commission for development purposes
    (c) Twelfth Finance Commission grants passed on by the State Government.
    (d) Untied grants for local planning.
    (e) Grants in respect of Centrally Sponsored Schemes that have been assigned to the local bodies for the purposes of implementation.
    (f) Grants for State Plan schemes assigned for implementation through Local Governments.
    (g) Grants for Externally supported schemes assigned for implementation through Local Governments.
    (h) Estimated contribution by the communities themselves.

12. The DPC will consolidate the two streams – the Panchayat plans and the urban area plans, integrate them with the departmental plans for the district and prepare the draft five year plan and the Annual Plan.

13. The State Planning Commission/Board/Department may issue the above as guidelines and suggest the broad structure of the district plan document and the forms to be annexed to the document.

V Presentation as part of State's Eleventh Plan Proposals:

1. A summary of the District Plans will have to be presented as part of the State's Eleventh Five Year and Annual (2007-08) Plan proposals.
2. For this purpose, a Note on the present status of empowerment of local governments and the procedures adopted in getting local draft plans prepared by all levels of local governments will be attached to the plan proposals.
3. Summary statements will be presented in the attached Annexure-III formats in addition to the forms usually adopted for State Plan Proposals. (The forms refer to Annual Plan could be the same for five year plan).
4. The sum total of the outlay on District Plans in a state may be around 40 percent of the gross state plan outlay".

Source: No. M-13011/1/2006-SP-Coord. Planning Commission (State Plans Division).

Appendices - 3.1

Planning Commission
(MIP Division)
Subjects: Backward Districts Initiative- Rastriya Sam Vikas Yojana
The Scheme and Guidelines for Preparation of District Plans

The Scheme

The Backward Districts Initiative under the Rashtriya Sam Vikas Yojana has been initiated with the main objective of putting in place programmes and policies with the joint efforts of the Centre and the States which would remove barriers to growth, accelerate the development process and improve the quality of life of the people. The scheme aims at focused development programmes for backward areas which help reduce imbalances and speed up development.

This component will cover 100 districts. The identification of backward districts within a State has been made on the basis of an index of backwardness comprising three parameters with equal weights to each: (i) value of output per agriculture worker (ii) agriculture wage rate; and (iii) percentage of SC. ST population of the districts. The number of districts per State has been worked out on the basis of incidence of poverty (list of districts at Annex-I). In addition, thirty two-districts which are affected by Left Wing Extremism will also be covered

(Annexure-II). Fifty Backward Districts and 16 districts affected by Left Wing Extremism are being covered in Annual Plan 2003-04.

The main objectives of the scheme are to address the problems of low agricultural productivity, unemployment and to fill critical gaps in physical and social infrastructure. The District Administration Panchayati Raj Institutions accordingly would be required to prepare a Three- Year Master Plan with nested Annual Action Plans. The Plan is to be based on a SWOT (Strengths, Weaknesses, Opportunities and Threats) Analysis, review of ongoing schemes and identification of a few lead sectors wherein state intervention would help the district overcome major bottlenecks in development.

The additionality is to be used to meet local needs through schemes in these lead sectors which would make a dent on the poverty of the district in a time bound manner.

Release of Funds

A sum of Rs. 15.00 crore per year will be provided to each of the districts for a period of three years i.e. a total of Rs. 45.00 crore per district. funds will be released to the State Governments on 100 per cent grant basis in suitable instalments linked with the satisfactory progress of the District Plan.

The State Government will release the funds received under the programme to a separate head created for the purpose under the District Rural Development Agency within 15 days of the receipt of the said funds. Failure to do so will lead to forfeiture of subsequent instalments and the funds release earlier being treated as a loan.

Delivery Mechanism

- There is a High Level Committee at the Government of India (GOI) level chaired by Deputy Chairman, Planning Commission with Finance Minister, Minister of State for Planning, Chief Minister, Government of Bihar, Chief Minister, Government of Orissa and Secretary, Planning

Commission as Members. This Committee will approve policies regarding initiatives of the Rashtriya Sam Vikas Yojana (RSVY), set the reform agenda for the State Governments and periodically conduct a review of the progress of the RSVY Programme.

- There is an Empowered Committee at the GOI level chaired by Secretary, Planning Commission which will approve the District Plans, monitor and review the programme, have evaluations and mid-term appraisals conducted and attend to all other matters relating to the operation of the RSVY.
- Each State Government has to set up a State Level Steering Committee under the Chairmanship of the State's Chief Secretary with about five other members.

  The Secretaries of the Departments of Finance and Planning, Chief Executive of the District (Deputy Commissioner or Chief Executive Officer of the Zilla Parishad), State Level representative of NABARD and in NGO could be members. In the case of districts affected by Left Wing Extremism, this Committee should also include the State's Home Secretary. The Committee would get detailed district plans prepared and recommend them to Planning Commission for concurrence of schemes. It would be also responsible for coordinating and ensuring synergy between departments and agencies as well as monitoring of the schemes.
- For each district the district plan should be prepared by a District Committee chaired by the District Magistrate CEO Zilla Parishad/ Chairperson of the District Planning Committee with the District Superintendent of Police (in case of Extremist-affected districts), District Forest Officer, local NGO's other stakeholders, etc., as members.

Guidelines for Preparation of District Plans

For availing of assistance under the Scheme, a three-year Master Plan is to be prepared for each district with nested Annual Action Plan.

The main Principles which have to be taken into consideration are:

1. The flow of funds from all sources namely State Plan, Centrally sponsored schemes, Central Schemes, externally aided projects etc., are to be indicated along with the specific schemes for the additionality under the Rashtriya Sam Vikas Yojana.
2. Funds under the RSVY are to be used as an additionality only for those schemes for which funding from other sources including State Plan, Centrally Sponsored Schemes, Central Schemes, etc., is not available.
3. The cost effectiveness of all schemes should be carefully considered so that returns from the funds invested under the scheme are maximized.
4. Peoples participation and involvement of PRLs, NGOs and Self Help Groups should be ensured at every stage including plan formulation, implementation and monitoring.
5. PRLs, NGOs and Self Help Groups may also be involved in awareness and capacity building training etc, and about two per cent of the funds could be utilized for such schemes.
6. Employment related schemes and vocational training need special attention specially in the districts affected by Left Wing Extremism. However, schemes for self-employment may be based on credit rather than subsidy. Therefore, each project should be a bankable enterprise and subject to appraisal and banking discipline. The enterprises should be promoted through private/group initiatives and not through the government/ government sponsored Cooperative sector. Funds should not be provided to prop up ailing government/ government sponsored cooperative enterprises. The aim is to encourage self employment programmes for income generating activities through small assistance to Self-Help Groups towards revolving fund and provision of the required infrastructure and training imputes.

7. Subsidy linked schemes may be allowed only if absolutely essential as a supplemental measure for expanded coverage of a Central/State Plan ;scheme and subsidy should be kept at the same level as that provided in the case of similar Central Government Schemes. For schemes involving creation of community assets efforts should be made to ensure a beneficiary contribution wherever feasible.
8. Allocation under RSVY may be made only after exhausting in full the assistance available under various Centrally Sponsored/ Central Plan/ State Plan schemes including those under KVIC, PMRY, SGSY, SJSRY, etc.
9. Funds under RSVY should not be used for acquisition of land for any project, construction or renovation of administrative bullrings, establishment costs/staff costs, and other such schemes. No new posts are to be created for this programme.
10. There should be complete transparency in the choice of schemes and their locations. The prioritized list of schemes and the reasons for taking up the schemes and the criteria for choice of locations must be made available on the web-site. Similarly all tenders should be on the web-site.
11. All schemes are to be completed within the prescribed three-year time frame. No cost over-run will be permitted.
12. It should be ensured that the schemes are sustainable and assets should be planned with care so that they are useful and maintained even after the scheme is over. Special attention is to be given to sustainability of each project. In the case of community assets, wherever possible future maintenance should be built into the programme, e.g. if a community hall is constructed, individuals who use the hall should be charged so that a corpus fund for maintenance can be set up.
13. Efforts should be made to concentrate on the poorer pockets and the disadvantaged communities within the district.

14. The Plan should be based on vision for the district and not be a mere collection of schemes for which funding from existing sources is insufficient.

Steps for the preparation of District Plan

The first step would be to conduct a stock taking of the existing situation in the district namely: a resource inventory existing flow of funds for various schemes, strengths of the district, identification of critical gaps and drawing up a scheme to fill these gaps. In this exercise the PRIs and NGOs should be involved. The potential linked credit plan of the district prepared by NABARD may be used while preparing the district plan to ensure higher flow of credit to the district. The Institution identified for undertaking benchmark surveys/ monitoring should be directed to undertake the benchmark survey for critical indicators.

The Plan should be drawn up as per the Chapter scheme given below and got approved by the State level Steering Committee in consultation with the Pr. Adviser/ Adviser from Planning Commission who has been assigned the district.

The Plan is to be sent to Planning Commission where it will be examined by the subject Divisions concerned and either sent back for modification or put up to the Empowered Committee for approval. After the approval of the Empowered Committee and receipt of summary record, the State may sign the MOA and send it to the Planning Commission for signatures. A copy of the signed MOA will be sent to the State Government and the first instalment of funds will be released for the district.

Chapter Scheme

Each district plan should contain an executive summary highlighting district specific problems and suggested strategy. Each Plan document should have the following Chapters:

1. Background
2. Resource Inventory
3. SWOT analysis and listing of critical gaps

4. Summary of Objectives/ Benefits expected to be achieved after three years.
5. Schematic details including time and cost schedules quarter-wise.
6. Benchmark Surveys. Monitoring and Concurrent Evaluation.
7. Annexes.

Source: website of the Planning Commission

Appendices - 3.2

The Planning Process for Backward Region Grant Fund (BRGF)

2.1. Each Panchayat or Municipality within the backward district concerned will be the unit for planning under BRGF. Plans prepared by each Panchayat or Municipality will be consolidated into the District plan by the District Planning Committee, constituted in accordance with Article 243ZD of the Constitution. The planning exercise will be done in accordance with the guidelines issued by the Planning Commission from time to time. The current guidelines for the preparation of the district plans issued by the Planning Commission, in respect of annual planning and the 11th Five Year Plan are placed at Annexe. 2. (shown here at Appendix: 3.1)

2.2. Ensuring the inclusion of disadvantaged groups during the consolidation of District plans in accordance with the Vision set out in the Planning Commission's guidelines: In keeping with the 'Vision' set out in the Planning Commission's guidelines, during consolidation of plans, particular care shall be taken to ensure that the district plan addresses issues relating to SC/ ST development. In this direction, the following may be fully addressed:

(a) A separate sub-plan should be prepared, within the plan of each Panchayat and ULB, showing the scheme-wise allocations for SCs/STs,

(b) Schemes benefiting SCs/STs should be allocated funds at least in proportion to the population of these communities in the jurisdiction for which the plan has been prepared.

(c) Amenities such as schools, anganwadis, health centers etc., should be provided on priority in those villages that have a substantial SC/ST population.

Source: Website of the Ministry of Rural Development, GoI.

Appendices - 3.3

Guidelines of Planning under REGS

PLANNING

3.1.1 Planning is critical to the successful implementation of the Rural Employment Guarantee Scheme (REGS). A key indicator of success is the timely generation of employment within 15 days while ensuring that the design and selection of works are such that good quality assets are developed. The need to act within a time limit necessitates advance planning. The basic aim of the planning process is to ensure that the District is prepared well in advance to offer productive employment on demand.

3.1.2 Section 16(4) of the Act requires the Gram Panchayats to forward proposals for REGS projects to the Programme Officer for scrutiny and preliminary approval prior to the commencement of the year in which these projects are to be executed.

3.1.3 The Programme Officer is responsible, under Section 15(3) of the Act, for matching the demand for work in the Block with the employment opportunities arising from REGS projects. For this purpose, he/she is expected, under Section 15(4), to prepare a plan for the Block by consolidating the proposals of the Gram Panchayats and the Intermediate Panchayats. Under Section 13(3), the Intermediate Panchayat has to approve and forward the Block Plan to the District Panchayat.

3.1.4 Under Section 14(6) of the Act, the District Programme Coordinator is required to prepare a 'labour budget' by the end of December for the next financial year.

This labour budget should contain the details of the anticipated demand for unskilled manual work in the District, and the plan for engagement of labourers in REGS works. It should be submitted to the District Panchayat.

3.1.5 The need to coordinate different levels of planning, and to prepare a 'shelf of projects' to offer employment on demand, requires the preparation of an Annual The National Rural Employment Guarantee Act, 2005 Plan for the District. This should be done well before the commencement of the year in which the works are to be executed.

3.1.6 The Annual Plan will be like a rolling plan, since the approved shelf of projects will carry over from one financial year to the next. Thus, the Annual Plan cannot be seen in discrete terms. Rather, it should be seen as part of a longer-term strategy for sustainable employment generation in the District. The need to integrate work priorities with a longer-term development strategy is reflected in Schedule I of the Act, which states that the 'creation of durable assets and strengthening the livelihood resource base of the rural poor shall be an important objective of the Scheme'. It is suggested, therefore, that Districts develop Perspective Plans to enable them to assess the causal factors of poverty and possible interventions.

3.1.7 The State Council is expected to prepare a list of preferred works for different areas based on their ability to create durable assets.

3.2 THE DISTRICT PERSPECTIVE PLAN

3.2.1 The District Perspective Plan (DPP) is intended to facilitate advance planning and to provide a development perspective for the District. The aim is to identify the types of REGS works that should be encouraged in the District, and the potential linkages between these works and long-term employment generation and sustained development. Guidelines for the preparation of District Perspective Plans will be provided separately.

3.2.2 A District Perspective Plan of five years will have the advantage of facilitating annual working plans on the basis of which annual budgets can be estimated and drawn up, and also give a continuum to plan works beyond the restriction of a financial year. The District Perspective Plan will serve as a framework of long-term planning, but it will be flexible enough to respond to the new emerging needs of the area, the experience of implementation, and the new works approved by the Central Government.

3.2.3 Generally, a District Perspective Plan will have the following features:

(a) Village-based: with the village as the unit for planning;

(b) Holistic: cover socio-economic aspects of development;

(c) Diagnostic: include a causal analysis of poverty. This will help identify gaps and needs, and indicate the nature of inputs required.

(d) Delineate baselines;

(e) Indicate outcome-based strategies;

(f) Indicate methods for measurement of outcomes; and

(g) Map resources.

3.2.4 The District Perspective Plan will enable the adoption of a project approach to works rather than just an activity approach. It will also facilitate an inter-sectoral approach, so that Districts can address certain fundamental causes of poverty in the area.

3.2.5 If the Perspective Plan has been made under the National Food for Work Programme (NFFWP), it should be revisited in order to serve the purposes of NREGA. Forthis purpose, the draft Plan should be discussed and approved, with modifications if need be, by the Gram Sabha, Gram Panchayat, Intermediate Panchayat and District Panchayat. At the village level, efforts should be made to ensure the participation of those who are likely to seek work under the Act. Their demand for work as well as their preference for the nature and time of work should be elicited, so that the Plan becomes an instrument to give them employment according to their need. Each village should develop its Perspective Plan, so that it can benchmark the incremental improvements associated with REGS.

3.3 THE ANNUAL PLAN

3.3.1 The Annual Plan will be the working plan that identifies the activities to be taken up on priority in a year. The Perspective Plan will provide the framework for facilitating this identification. If new activities need to be taken up, their justification should be indicated in terms of needs and outcomes. The process for this will be as stipulated in the Act, based on the participation of the community, with a principal role assigned to the Panchayats.

3.3.2 Every year the Gram Panchayat shall convene a meeting of the Gram Sabha to estimate the demand for labour, and to propose the number and priority of works to be taken up in the next financial year. The timing of the meeting will take into consideration the work season and the migration time, in case the workforce in that area tends to migrate for work. Participation of likely beneficiaries should be ensured in the Gram Sabha so that their priorities and needs shape the Annual Plan. The time and date of the Gram Sabha meeting should be fixed well in advance and should be widely publicized so that people can participate in large numbers.

3.3.3 The recommendations formulated in the Gram Sabha (and the Ward Sabhas, if applicable) will be forwarded to the

Gram Panchayat. Based on these recommendations, the Gram Panchayat will prepare an Annual Plan and forward it to the Programme Officer. The Annual Plan should indicate clearly the existing demand for work, the demand in the previous year, the works taken up in the previous year, ongoing works and works proposed for the next year, likely costs and the proposed Implementing Agencies. The Gram Panchayat will also identify the 50 per cent of the works in its area that it may wish to take up.

Source: Website of the Ministry of Rural Development.

Appendices - 3.4

Guidelines of Planning under NREGA, 2005

PLANNING

The National Rural Employment Guarantee Act, 2005

3.3.4 The Programme Officer will scrutinize the Annual Plan for its technical feasibility. He will satisfy himself that it meets the likely demand for employment based on the registrations and previous experience. He will ascertain that the employment opportunities arising from the projects in the area under his jurisdiction match the demand for employment. If the Programme Officer feels that the list is insufficient to meet the likely demand, he should ask for a supplementary list.

3.3.5 The Programme Officer will not reject a proposal received from the Gram Panchayat. If the proposal is not within the parameters of the Act, or appears technically unfeasible, the Programme Officer will record his observations on the proposal and then submit a consolidated statement of proposals to the Intermediate Panchayat. The Intermediate Panchayat will not reject a work proposed by the Gram Panchayat if it is within the parameters of the Act. If it is outside the parameters of the Act, then it will be returned to the Gram Panchayat for this body to replace it with a valid proposal.

3.3.6 The Intermediate Panchayat will maintain the priority indicated by the Gram Panchayat. It is possible that there may be a need for works that involve more than one Gram Panchayat. Such works may be included by the Intermediate Panchayat. It is, however, reiterated that the priority of works in a Gram Panchayat will be as determined by the Gram Panchayat. On the basis of these discussions, the plan for the area of the Intermediate Panchayat will be approved by the Intermediate Panchayat and forwarded to the District Programme Coordinator.

3.3.7 The District Programme Coordinator will scrutinize the plan proposals of all the Intermediate Panchayats, examining the appropriateness and adequacy of works in terms of likely demand as well as their technical and financial feasibility. He/she will also invite and examine work proposals from other Implementing Agencies, but in doing so, the priorities of the Gram Panchayat and the priorities of inter Gram Panchayat works as indicated in the Block Plan by the Intermediate Panchayat will be retained. He/she will consolidate all these proposals into a District Plan proposal to be discussed and approved by the District Panchayat. The time frame for each project must be specified in the Annual Plan. The District Plan will comprise a Block-wise shelf of projects. The Block-wise shelf of projects will be arranged Gram Panchayat-wise. The Implementing Agency for each work has to be identified keeping in view the mandatory minimum 50 per cent of the works to be executed by the Gram Panchayat. The District Panchayat will examine and approve the District Plan.

3.3.8 The District Programme Coordinator will coordinate the preparation of detailed technical estimates and sanctions. The project report of each approved work shall contain all details as may be specified in the technical/works manual of the State Government. It will also clarify the expected outcomes such as person days of employment, specifications of the physical assets (e.g. length of road, size of a tank) and enduring outcomes (e.g. area irrigated, villages connected).

3.3.9 The District Programme Coordinator will communicate the sanctioned Plan to the Programme Officer. The Programme Officer will forward a copy of the Block Plan with the shelf of projects to be executed in each Gram Panchayat as well as projects that may be inter Gram Panchayat. These will carry full project cost,time frame, person-days to be generated and the name of the Implementing Agency. Planning for projects must give priority to low-wage areas, where the demand for work at minimum wages is likely to be large. This process must be completed by December of the preceding year.

3.3.10 The State Government should prescribe the time frame for each level to propose, scrutinize and approve the works.

3.3.11 Approved works should be widely publicized.

Source: Website of the Ministry of Rural Development.

Appendices - 3.5

Guidelines of Planning under RKVY

The Planning Process of RKVY

3.1 Each District will formulate a District Agriculture Plan (DAP) by including the resources available from other existing schemes, District, State, or Central schemes such as BRGF, SGSY, NREGS and Bharat Nirman, etc. The District Agricultural Plans shall not be the usual aggregation of the existing schemes but would aim at moving towards projecting the requirements for development of Agriculture and allied sectors of the district. These plans will present the vision for Agriculture and allied sectors within the overall development perspective of the district. The District Agriculture Plans would present the financial requirement and the sources of financing the agriculture development plans in a comprehensive way. Since RKVY is conditional to proper District Planning and since Planning Commission has already circulated guidelines for District Planning in line with Constitutional requirements, these requirements should be adhered to by the state as far as possible. The states will have to specify the institutional mechanisms evolved by them for District Planning as resolved in the NDC and submit a status report at the stage of the Annual Plan exercise. The SLSC will monitor and ensure this.

The DAP will include animal husbandry and fishery, minor irrigation projects, rural development works, agricultural marketing schemes and schemes for water harvesting and conservation, etc., keeping in view the natural resources and technological possibilities in each district.

3.2 Each state will prepare a comprehensive State Agricultural Plan (SAP) by integrating the District Plans. The state will have to, at the outset, indicate resources that can flow from the state to the district. The DAP will integrate multiple programmes that are in operation in the district concerned, include the resources and activities indicated by the state, combine the resources available from the other programmes and finalize the plan. The elements that will be taken into account should cover at the very least

(a) Sectoral and District segments of the State Plan.

(b) Centrally sponsored schemes, viz., NREGS (National Rural Employment Guarantee Scheme), BRGF (Backward Region Grant Fund), SGSY (Swarn Jayanti Gram Swarojgar Yojana) and Bharat Nirman, etc. and

(c) Tied and untied grants from the Central and State Finance Commissions.

The preparation of the State Agricultural Plan could be a two-way process. In one method, the state nodal department (Agriculture Department) could obtain the draft DAPs from the districts in the first instance and examine if aspects of importance to the state are properly covered in the district plans or not. For example, at the state level, the vision could be to set up fertiliser quality testing labs in certain districts.

The state should, at this stage of scrutiny, ensure that establishment of the fertilizer testing labs is incorporated in the District Agricultural Plans of the districts concerned. Ensuring that the state's priorities with respect to Agriculture and allied sectors are appropriately captured in the District Agricultural Plans would be the responsibility of the nodal department/ State agency vested with the responsibility of preparing the SAPs. In the other method, the state Nodal Agency could communicate to the districts in the first instance, the state's priorities that ought to reflect in the respective district plans and the districts may incorporate these in their district plans. The preparation of the District Agriculture Plan is an elaborate, exhaustive and iterative process so every care should be taken by the state nodal department and the district agriculture department officials in ensuring that the DAPs are properly and comprehensively made.

3.3 Several states/UTs may already have prepared comprehensive district and state agriculture plans. They may ascertain if they could be updated and used for the purposes of the RKVY. However, in states with no such preparation, an exerciseshould immediately commence, so as to complete it within a three month period. The district level potential linked credit plans (PLP) already prepared by the NABARD may be useful in this regard. The state governments are advised to make best use of the PLPs and SREPs (Strategic Research and Extension Plans) developed under the ATMA programme. The guidelines for preparing the District Development Plans have been communicated to the state governments by the Planning Commission. For the purpose of the RKVY, the District Development Plans so prepared, in accordance with the Planning Commission's Guidelines should be broadly sufficient. It should however be ensured that the convergence with other programmes as well as the role assigned to the PRIs are satisfactory. For the year 2007-08, a clear indication should be given by the states that they are encouraging the preparation of the district agriculture plans that are integral to the District

Development Plan. The intent of the states will be known by the number of districts already covered, and the availability of a road map for covering the remaining districts. Eventually, i.e., from 2008-09 onwards, no assistance under the RKVY shall be available unless all the districts are ready with the District Plans Programmes.

Illustration

District Rural Development Programmes

District Agriculture Plan

District Animal Husbandry, Dairying and Fisheries Programmes

Other Departmental Programmes such as soil and water conservation, etc.

Wherever the states feel the need to engage consultants to prepare the DAP and/or

SAP, they may do so.

3.4 The finalized State Agriculture Plan will be placed before the Department of Agriculture (DAC) and the Planning Commission, as a part of the State Plan exercise, for Additional Central Assistance by the State Planning Department. The DAC and Planning Commission will approve the SAP with such suggestions as may be necessary. The states will provide complete rationale and justification for the assistance sought, well before the state plan discussions to give sufficient time to the DAC and the Planning Commission to firm up their views on the proposals and make such consultations as may be necessary with concerned departments.

3.5 The districts will be required to prepare a shelf of projects, for posing to the SLSC under Stream-I. At least 75% of the total funds under the RKVY that a state gets entitled to, will be available under the Stream-I. The Nodal Department/Agency will undertake/compile such projects from each of the districts ,prioritize them and place them before the SLSC. The SLSC is vested with the authority to sanction the projects under Stream-I in a meeting that will be attended by representatives of the Government of India. The Nodal Agency will give at least 15 clear days of notice to the representatives of the Government of India while sending the meeting notice, along with a gist of the agenda. The projects posed to the SLSC under Stream-I shall be consistent with the District and State Agriculture Plans. The balance of the total RKVY funds will be available for strengthening of the existing schemes and for filling resource gaps under the State Plans. This would be untied assistance to the states.

3.6 A state is permitted to use upto 1% of its total RKVY funds for incurring administrative expenditure, which includes payments to consultants, recurring expenses of various kinds, staff costs, etc. However, no permanent employment can be created, nor can vehicles be purchased.

3.7 The DAC may retain a proportion of 1% of the RKVY funds at its level, so as to organize pan-India evaluations or for such administrative contingencies that may arise at various times.

Source: Website of the Ministry of Rural Development.

Appendices - 3.6

Guidelines of Planning under Prime Ministers Gram Sadak Yojana (PMGSY)

4. Planning for Rural Roads

4.1 Proper planning is imperative to achieve the objectives of the Programme in a systematic and cost effective manner. The Manual for the Preparation of District Rural Roads Plan and the Core Network, shall be treated as part of the Guidelines and would stand amended to the extent modified by the present Guidelines. The Manual lays down the various steps in the planning process and the role of different Agencies including the Intermediate Panchayat, the District Panchayat as well as the State Level Standing Committee. In the identification of the Core Network, the priorities of elected representatives, including MPs and MLAs, are expected to be duly taken into account and given full consideration. The Rural Roads Plan and the Core Network would constitute the basis for all planning exercises under the PMGSY.

4.2 The District Rural Roads Plan would indicate the entire existing road network system in the District and also clearly identify the proposed roads for providing connectivity to Unconnected Habitations, in an economic and efficient manner in terms of cost and utility. The Core **Network** will identify the roads required to assure each eligible habitation with a basic access (single all-weather road connectivity) to essential social and economic services. Accordingly, the Core Network would consist of some of the existing roads as well as all the roads proposed for new construction under the PMGSY.

4.3 In proposing the new links under the District Rural Roads Plan, it would be first necessary to indicate the weightage for various services. The District Panchayat shall be the competent authority to select the set of socio-economic / infrastructure variables best suited for the District, categorise them and accord relative weightages to them. This would be communicated to all concerned before commencing the preparation of the District Rural Roads Plan.

4.4 The Plan would first be prepared at the Block level, in accordance with the directions contained in the Manual and the priorities spelt out by the District Panchayat. In short, the existing road network would be drawn up, unconnected habitations identified and the roads required to connect these unconnected habitations prepared. This shall constitute the Block Level Master Plan.

4.5 Once this exercise is completed, the Core Network for the Block is identified, by making best use of the existing and proposed road facilities in such a manner that all the eligible habitations are assured of a basic access. It must be ensured that every eligible habitation is within 500 metres (1.5 km of Path length in the Hills) of a connected habitation or an All-weather road (either existing or planned). In drawing up the proposed road links, the requirements of the people must be taken into account, through the socio-economic / infrastructure values (Road Index) suitably weighted (see Para 4.3) and the alignment having the higher Road Index ought to be considered for selection.

4.6 The Block level Master Plan and the Core Network are then placed before the Intermediate Panchayat for consideration and approval of the Core Network. They are simultaneously sent, along with the list of all unconnected habitations to the Members of Parliament and MLAs, for their comments, if any. After approval by the Intermediate Panchayat, the Plans would be placed before the District Panchayat for its approval. It will be incumbent on the District Panchayat to ensure that the suggestions given by the Members of Parliament are given full consideration within the framework of these Guidelines. Once approved by the District Panchayat, a copy of the Core Network would be sent to the State-level Agency as well as the National Rural Roads Development Agency. No road work may be proposed under the PMGSY for New Connectivity or Upgradation (where permitted) unless it forms part of the Core Network.

Source: Website of the Ministry of Rural Development.

Index

R

T

U

V

W

Z